RESEARCH METHODS
AND STATISTICS

RESEARCH METHODS AND STATISTICS

Jeremy Miles

First published in 2001 by Crucial, a division of Learning Matters Ltd.

British Library Cataloguing in Publication Data
A CIP record for this book is available from the British Library.

ISBN 1 903337 15 1

Crucial
58 Wonford Road
Exeter EX2 4LQ
Tel: 01392 215560
Email: info@crucial.uk.com
www.crucial.uk.com

Cover design by Topics – The Creative Partnership
Project Management by Deer Park Productions
Typeset by PDQ Typesetting
Printed and bound in Great Britain by Bell & Bain Ltd., Glasgow

Contents

....

Contents

Preface and Acknowledgements

You probably are not very interested in learning about research methods and statistics. But if you are studying psychology at university, it is a subject that you need to cover. You need to read textbooks in order to carry out the work that is assigned to you, and to pass (and hopefully do well) in examinations. However, few textbooks seem to acknowledge that fact. Most are written as if you are reading them because you would like to know more about the subject. Very few people read statistics books because they are interested in them – they read them because they have to. (I should point out that I am an exception to this – I am told, very specifically, by my wife that I was to remove all statistics books from my suitcase when we go on holiday, because 'they are not holiday reading'.)

In this book I have tried to take a different approach – I have tried to write a book that acknowledges that you are studying research methods and statistics because you have to, not because you want to. The book focuses on the type of assessment that you will undergo at university, and concentrates on what you need to know and do, in order to do well in those assessments.

It is my hope, however, that by reading this book you will realise that research methods and statistics are not something that you are required to suffer, but something that you can enjoy – and who knows, you might be taking research methods and statistics books on holiday with you sometime.

Although this book has my name on the cover, it would not have ever come into being if it were not for the efforts of a lot of other people. First, Jonathan Harris and Mandy Preece at Learning Matters, for having the idea in the first place, and providing the guidance necessary to improve the quality of the book. Also to all those people who have taken it upon themselves to plough through earlier drafts and versions. These people (in no particular order) are Susanne Hempel (Derby University, the aforementioned long-suffering wife), Diane Miles (the probably longer suffering mother), Phil Banyard (Nottingham Trent University), Mark Torrance (Staffordshire University) and Linden Ball (Lancaster University) who assisted with parts of the section on report writing. In addition, I would like to thank the psychology students at Derby University who took the time to read through and comment on early drafts – Gemma Seymour, Kirsten Lee and Lisa Janiec. Finally, I would like to thank Ian Toone, from Cannock College, much of this book was inspired by what I learned from him.

Of course, despite these people's best efforts, I have probably managed to slip in some errors, and any book I have produced will never be free of faults. If you find anything you believe to be in error, or if you have any other comments, of any kind, on the book, please feel free to contact me at jeremy@jeremymiles.co.uk, or the website at http://www.jeremymiles.co.uk/crucial.

STUDYING AND LEARNING ABOUT
STUDYING AND LEARNING ABOUT
RESEARCH METHODS AND STATISTICS

Chapter summary

In this introduction we will have a look at why we need to cover research methods and statistics as part of your psychology degree. We will also have a look at some of the different methods of assessment that you are likely to encounter, and have a long look at the main method of assessment in research methods and statistics: the practical report.

Section I   Why do I need to know this stuff?

You came to university to learn about psychology. You thought you would learn about people and their behaviour. Perhaps you thought that you would learn a little about yourself, or your friends and family. You might want to work in an area of applied psychology, such as clinical psychology, counselling psychology or occupational psychology. You might not want to work in psychology itself, but see psychology as being a useful subject to have studied in your planned career in market research, advertising, teaching or any one of a large number of jobs.

But when you get to university to study psychology, you find that you need to study research methods and statistics. So why, you might ask.

There are several good answers to that question.

Because you have to

In the UK, the British Psychological Society (BPS) recognises psychology degrees. Many jobs and postgraduate training courses specify that you should have studied a degree that is recognised by the BPS. The BPS specify certain criteria that a psychology graduate should satisfy – and one of these criteria is a knowledge of research methods and statistics.

Of course the BPS don't insist upon you studying research methods and statistics just to be unpleasant or cruel – they have very good reasons for insisting, and we will look at these reasons now.

Understanding and evaluating research

In your psychology degree, you will spend a great deal of time reading about research. In order to read about research with understanding, you need to understand the research process – and so you need to study research methods. You must be able to differentiate good research from bad research (or more likely, good research from OK research or speculation).

If you go on to work in any applied field in psychology, you need to be able to evaluate research findings. If you are working as a counselling psychologist you will read about research findings, and you need to decide whether those findings are built on firm methodological foundations. In addition, you might need to understand why your own hunches and feelings about what works and what does not work are not necessarily correct.

If you do not go on to work in an area of psychology, you will still find that you will use the skills that you have gained through studying research methods. Almost any job that you end up doing will require you to evaluate findings and data that are presented to you. Having studied research methods, you will be able to make better decisions based on those data.

Crucial tip	The word 'data' is plural. The singular of the word 'data' is 'datum'. You should always write 'the data are...' not 'the data is...'. (See how often you can catch your tutors making this mistake.)

Carrying out research

After your psychology degree, you might go on into a career of research and if this is your intention, then it is obvious why you should study research methods. All kinds of organisations that you might work for in the future carry out research. A commercial enterprise wants research done to find out levels of customer satisfaction. Police authorities do a large amount of research – they look into and evaluate different policing methods, so that they can make decisions about how they should operate and these decisions will then be based on evidence, not just hunches.

Hospitals carry out research looking at patient satisfaction and examining what changes should be made that might improve that satisfaction. Banks and loan companies carry out research to examine what kind of people pay back their loans, and what kind of people do not, so that they can place their money with the least risk of losing it on a bad debt.

Enjoyable

It is now that you will think that I am completely mad, but bear with me for a moment, and I will try to explain. If you know about research methods, you can carry out research, and carrying out research can be, for want of a better word, fun.

If you study psychology, you may well come across questions that no one has tried to answer. You might think of a novel way of answering that question. You design a study that, you think, will answer that question, and then you carry out your research. You analyse your results and find that you have the answer to the question that your research was designed to find out. Finally, you write the report. You will have added to the knowledge of psychology.

So why is it so hard?

Learning about research methods and statistics is hard. And it can be boring – although usually it is boring because it is hard.

It is hard because there are a large number of ingredients to a research study, which need to be put together properly. In this way, carrying out psychological research is a little like cooking. To cook a recipe you have to follow the correct steps, in the correct order. If you get one step wrong, they recipe will not work. There are therefore two ways of learning about research methods and statistics.

The first way to learn about research methods and statistics is the 'cookbook approach'. If we were using the cookbook approach to teaching you research methods and statistics we would describe the recipe for each procedure (or food) that you wanted to make, and you would follow it, to the letter. There are two problems with the cookbook approach. The first is that if something does not go according to plan, you do not know what to do. I had a friend who regularly made scones, according to a recipe. The recipe book said to cook the scones for 15 minutes, but the scones were always undercooked and soggy in the middle. Because my friend always followed the recipe, to the letter, they could not adapt the recipe and cook them properly. The second problem is that you need to learn an awful lot of different recipes. You need to learn the recipe for cheese and onion pie, jam tarts, sausage rolls and apple turnovers all separately. But the basic recipe for each of these is the same – make some pastry, put something in it. Just change the shape and the filling.

Therefore, a better approach to the cookbook approach is to teach you about the principles of designing research. However, here we strike another problem – there are a lot of steps to take to design a research study, and before you can go ahead you need to understand each of these steps, and you have to get every step right. The same is true for cooking, but we don't realise it. Imagine an alien from another planet trying to understand something as simple as cooking potatoes. 'So, I peel them, and then put them in the oven. Oh, with oil. But if I don't peel them I don't need oil. Or I peel them and put them in a saucepan. With water. Or I chop them and put them in a saucepan, with oil. But I can chop them before I put them in the water.' Imagine the disaster if the alien forgot the water in the saucepan.

Section 2: Learning about research methods and statistics in psychology

Taking responsibility

You will find studying at degree level somewhat different from your previous educational experiences: you are not guided along a well-trodden trail (though you should get direction and encouragement). The main difference is that with a certain amount of help and encouragement, you have to work out your own path, and use your own initiative and self-discipline to replace constant supervision. Your lecturers will not shout at you if you do not do the work that is required. You will simply fail.

Crucial tip	To remind yourself of your responsibilities, cut the following figure out of this book and tape it to the mirror in your bathroom where you will see it every morning. (If you don't want to damage the book, you can photocopy it.)

The person you are looking at will determine how well you do in your psychology degree.

Many students find this thought a little scary. Your education is now down to you. Whether you succeed or fail depends on what you do. Of course, this was always true in the past. Whether you succeeded or failed at school or college was also down to you, but at school or college, as long as you listened to what your teachers said, and did pretty much what they told you to do, you will have been OK. At university, this is not enough any more. You are now expected to take more responsibility for your learning – it is, after all, your degree: you have to take responsibility for it.

Managing your time

You will find when you go to university that you seem to have a lot of time to do what you want to do – you are not expected to spend a great deal of time in lectures or seminars. You can (and should and will) spend some of that time doing all sorts of things your parents would disapprove of and which you will not get the chance to do again. You will watch daytime television. You will stay up talking to your friends until it is light outside, and then you will sleep all day. You will eat only toast for days on end. You will do the kind of things that I am not going to write about in this kind of book.

But while you are doing all of those things, you need to think about the fact that you want to pass your degree – you probably want to do more than pass, you want to do well, and to get a good degree you need to spend some time studying. Actually, you need to spend quite a lot of time studying. This doesn't need to get in the way of doing other things – there are 168 hours in a week, and you will spend about 56 of those hours sleeping. That leaves 113 hours to divide between your studies and things that you want to do.

At university, deadlines tend to be very strict. At the start of your course, you will probably have been told about the deadlines for work that you need to submit - perhaps this information was given to you in a course handbook or a module handbook or even on a piece of paper. It is quite likely that no one will remind you that the work needs to be completed, until it is due to be handed in. In addition, unlike at school or college, it needs to be handed in – not the day after the deadline, not five minutes after the deadline but absolutely before the deadline. And if you try to work at the last minute: your computer will crash, the library will be shut, you will run out of ink – so prepare yourself to be ready well ahead of deadlines. When you were at school, your teachers were likely to be sympathetic if your computer crashed and wiped out the essay just before you printed it. At university you will be asked why you didn't have a back-up.

Following instructions

In lectures, in handouts and on the Internet, you will find instructions. These instructions will tell you what to do, and often when to do it; they will also provide you with ideas for background reading, suggest where to find help if you are stuck, and give lots of other useful information. You need to read any instructions extremely carefully. If you skim them and do not absorb the details, you may end up having to say 'Oh, but I didn't know that I was supposed to do that, I didn't read it…' Your lecturers are likely to have little sympathy with you.

Crucial tip	It may seem like you have an awful lot of information to absorb, but it is worth trying to absorb it. If you waste your tutors' time with questions to which you have the answers in your materials, your tutors will not be pleased with you. RTFM,* as they say.
	* Read The Fine Manual (or something like that).

Arranging to study

At university, you will need to spend more time studying on your own. You need to plan *where, when* and *how*. It is very important to choose somewhere suitable to study. You need to find a place where you have some space and where you can concentrate. Spending time studying in the communal areas is more fun than studying on your own, but if you cannot concentrate then that study time is not of much value. If you want to be with other people, you should be with other people properly, and not be glancing at a book. If you want to study, do that properly too. I don't need to tell you that you should:

- avoid having to study when you are too tired to concentrate properly;
- select the studying times best suited to you;
- set yourself time targets for studying – you need to take breaks to remain fresh.

Learning from textbooks

As a university student, you will be expected to spend a lot more time learning from books. You will probably buy a textbook on research methods and statistics, and you may use other books in the library.

Studying from books on research methods and statistics is a little bit different from studying other areas of psychology. Most textbooks cover very similar material – most of the sections you find in one textbook on research methods and statistics you will find in all. You will not need to spend time searching for a book that has the material that you need in order to answer a particular question. However, it is still a good idea to look in different textbooks, even though they cover the same material: you might find that when you read some material in one book, it does not make sense to you, but by reading it in a second book, it becomes clearer. Often there are many different ways of explaining concepts in research methods, you might find that if it is explained to you one way, it does not make sense, but if it is explained a second way, the parts of the jigsaw might start to fit together and it will make more sense.

USING YOUR BOOK

If you have bought a book, it is your book. You should use it as your book. If you want or need to resell it, you might be tempted to try to keep the book in as near-new a condition as possible: but then why did you buy it? Books are there to be read, and that means they must suffer some wear and tear. While you might be able to recover some of the cost of your book by reselling it, you really want to get everything that you can from the book. Use a highlighter pen, and make notes in the margins. You may find that if you do this, it will help to identify these key areas, and helps you access them quickly and easily, and it helps you remember and apply the information. (If you ever see my bookshelves, it is very easy to see the books that I like – they look old and battered, and they are full of notes, marks, highlights and have post-it notes sticking out of different pages. The books I don't like are shiny and new.)

USING BOOKS

If you want to do well in your degree, you will need to refer to journal articles and a range of books as well as your own textbook. In research methods and statistics you will need to use journals less and books more. In this section, I will give you some advice about how to approach reading a journal article or section of a textbook.

Cognitive psychologists talk of people as being 'cognitive misers' or say that people are 'cognitively lazy'. They mean that our brains are actually very lazy, and do not want to do anything that they don't really have to do. (This is a good thing – one of the reasons why we humans are so clever at doing things is that our brain puts as little effort as possible into whatever it does: the result of this economising is that we have plenty of brain power remaining to do other things.) When you sit down to read a book, your brain probably doesn't want to read the book – it is rather mean with its energy and doesn't want to waste it on reading any boring old psychology textbook (especially a book on research methods). Everyone, on occasions, has had the experience of reading a book and finding that they get to a stage where they have no idea what has happened on the last few pages. Your brain switched off because it is lazy. Your brain thought to itself, 'I will just keep their eyes moving from side to side across the page, that will make them think that they are reading, and I will go and do something more interesting.' Sometimes you get to the stage where you can read and reread the same line three or four times, and yet your brain still will not take in the information. You need to do something that makes your brain carry on working.

One way to force your brain to keep concentrating is called the SQ3R technique. SQ3R stands for:

- Survey
- Question
- Read
- Review
- Recall.

We will have a look at these one at a time.

- *Survey.* This means to have a quick skim through the text, to see what it is going to tell you. At this stage you should be having an overall look at the text to see what it is going to be about. Look at the whole chapter or article to see what it is going to tell you.

To survey a chapter in a book	To survey a journal article
• Look at the subheadings. • Look at the figures, diagrams. • Read the chapter abstract (if there is one).	• Read the abstract. • Look at the subheadings. • Look at the tables or graphs in the results section. • Read the first paragraph of the introduction, and the first paragraph of the discussion, and maybe the last paragraph of the discussion.

- *Question.* Now, take one section at a time. In a journal article, the sections are likely to be the introduction, method, results and discussion. In a textbook the chapter will probably be divided into sections, each of which will have a subheading. Before you read each section, ask yourself what this section is going to tell you. Why did the author write this section? What will you learn from reading this section? How does this relate to what you already know?

- *Read.* The third stage is to read. Now read the section that you have asked yourself about. Keep the questions in mind as you read. It is probably better not to make notes at this stage, as making notes will distract you from reading and understanding what the text is saying.

- *Recall.* Now is the time to make notes. Try to recall the important parts of the section that you just read and write them down. Avoid the temptation of just copying from the text – if you do that, your brain will switch off again. Instead, write down the details in note format. If you can't remember something, go and read it again (but wait until you have finished reading before you start to make notes again).

- *Review.* Finally, you should review what you have learned. Test yourself to make sure that you have learned. If you aren't sure, or can't remember something, go back to your notes to check up on it.

The technique is summarised in diagrammatic form in Figure 1.

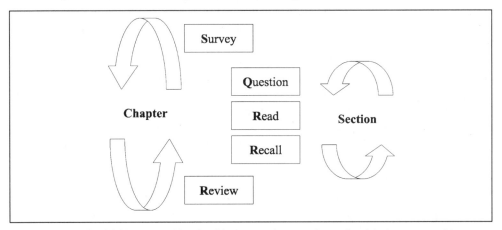

Figure 1: The SQ3R process. You should survey a chapter of a textbook before you read it. Then, when you approach each section, question what the section is about, read the section, and recall what you have just read. Do this for each section. When you have read all of the sections, you should review what the chapter was about. Then start again with the next chapter.

USING YOUR OLD BOOKS

If you have studied A-level or AS-level psychology, or psychology on an Access course, you may well have studied research methods and statistics as part of that course. You might have noticed that many of the topics that we cover here will be the same topics you covered on that course, and you might therefore be tempted to reuse your notes, and particularly your textbook. This is not a very good idea. (And not just in research methods and statistics – it is not a very good idea for any of your psychology work.)

It is not a *very* bad idea. Don't become downhearted if you were hoping to reuse these materials – just be aware of the drawback. And the drawback is that you will read the book, which has the same topics as your degree-level texts (many of the sections may even have the same headings) but they will not cover the information in the same detail. You might then find that you use the material in these lower-level books, and you do OK, but it is unlikely that you will ever do much better than OK – you need to 'step up a gear' and start using slightly more sophisticated thinking and approaches. I will give one example to demonstrate. If you are carrying out an experiment that incorporates a repeated measures design, you will be aware (if you have studied A-level) that you need to be aware of order effects, of which there are two types: practice effects and fatigue effects. You will also be aware that you need to counterbalance the order of the presentation to cancel out the order effects. Or so you would have been told, when you did A-level. If you turn to Chapter 3, you will see that we need to think about order effects slightly differently, and that counterbalancing will not necessarily solve the problems.

Section 3: Writing research reports in psychology

Introduction

If you have looked ahead, before you read this section (as suggested in the last section) you will notice that this section seems to be very long. Why such a long section on writing research reports? You know how to write an essay – writing a research report can't be so different from that? Well, no, it isn't, and yes, it is. Writing a research report is like writing anything else – you need to be clear in what you want to say, you need to argue your points well, and you need to use appropriate grammar and language. What is different about writing a practical report is that it has a very strict format and structure that you must follow. Psychology students often have difficulties adjusting to the strict format of a research report. Students with more of a scientific background tend to have difficulties with the prose sections. They want to make lists and organise the work very formally and tersely. This style is not appropriate for a psychology report. It must consist of proper prose throughout; never write in note form (however tempting that might be). Students with an arts or humanities background are not used to following the structure that is required. Everything you write must be in the correct place, and have the correct form. There is neither flexibility nor room for creativity in the practical report – you must adhere to the standard format.

I can't really emphasise enough how important it is to stick to the correct format – students lose marks, completely unnecessarily and frequently, because they don't stick to the correct format.

The format of the research report

The research reports that you write as a psychology student should look like professional journal articles in terms of their quality and structure. If you are in doubt about what a research report should look like or read like, then it helps to have a look through some psychology journals – this will give you some idea. However, you need to give slightly more information in your practical report than would be found in a journal article. You need to show your lecturers that you understand some aspects of research, and so your practical report will contain some additional sections and information that is not found in journal articles. If you are ever unsure what your report should look and read like, go and have a look at some journal articles.

This format or set of rules makes sure that empirical work is written about in clearly labelled sections, and each of these sections contains clearly defined chunks of information. You might notice that journal articles sometimes seem to break the rules that you will read here. They miss out sections, add sections or combine sections, because this makes the presentation of the research clearer. Sometimes you might think that it might be clearer to report your research if you break the rules in this way.

Crucial tip If you have read *The Growing Pains of Adrian Mole*, you might remember that Adrian sent one of his poems (about Norway) to the BBC. Adrian said that he had broken the rules of poetry in the same way that Picasso had broken the rules of painting. Someone at the BBC wrote back and told Adrian that 'before you can break the rules [of poetry] you do have to know what those rules are about' (Townsend, 1984, p. 76). Picasso could paint conventional art, and did, before he moved on to painting art that is more abstract. It might be better to break the rules with your research reports, but your lecturers, who will be assessing your work, want to find out at this point if you actually know the rules. So, don't break the rules – yet.

In general, the research report follows the order in which the work was carried out. Some parts of the report could have been written before the research was carried out, others could not have been written until afterwards. The Introduction and most of the Method section could be written before the research is carried out; the Results, Discussion and Abstract cannot be written until after the research has been carried out. Usually, the layout of the research report has these sections in this order:

Title
Abstract
Introduction
Method (comprising four subsections):
    Design
    Participants
    Materials
    Procedure
Results
Discussion
References
Appendices (if any)

> **Crucial tip**   When you write a report, make sure it has those sections, in that order. Surprisingly, students regularly lose marks for not doing this.

You should be aware that writing a good practical report takes a lot of time. It also requires a great deal of thinking time – which you may find you can do better if you are away from your desk.

The sections of the report

In this section, I will describe each part of the report and tell you what to put in each section. You should note that this is a general outline and that the demands of the report, or of your lecturers, may vary according to the type of study that you have carried out. However, before you move away from what it says in these guidelines, be very sure that you are doing the right thing.

TITLE

The title is the first part of the report that the person marking it will read, so you should try to ensure that you make a good first impression. The title should be as informative as you can make it, but no longer than one sentence, although you may include colons or semicolons. Good titles are important for someone searching the literature for relevant articles: the title will be the first thing a possible reader will use to decide whether to read further. Let the potential reader know the key issue of your piece of research. Never be vague. Do not, for example, title your report 'Memory' or 'An Experimental Investigation of Recall Aids' but something more specific like 'The Effect of the Method of Loci on the Recall of Unfamiliar Names.'

ABSTRACT

If someone has read the title of your report, the next thing they will do before they decide to take the time to read the whole thing is read the abstract. The abstract must provide enough information for someone to decide whether they want to read the whole report. As well as giving this information, you should try to keep the abstract as brief as possible. This whole section involves a compromise between informativeness and conciseness. An abstract should probably be around 150 words. You should not include minor or extraneous details (for example the sampling technique used) unless this is very important to the study.

In a published journal article, the abstract is placed onto databases that people use to search through the literature, such as PsycInfo.

INTRODUCTION

The introduction (obviously) exists to introduce your research. It should include the following parts:

- an account of the findings of relevant prior research and an overview of any particular conceptual issues that you think are important to your study;
- theoretical and practical aspects of your study.

Your introduction should be something like a short essay that brings together previous research on the subject, and concludes by saying what should be done next. Your study should almost 'fall out of' the end of your introduction. By the time the reader reaches the end of your introduction, you should have made it obvious that your research needs to be done.

When you state a fact in your introduction, you must cite evidence for it. The evidence is usually a piece of research. It is usually sufficient to identify a piece of research by the standard method of giving the name of the author and the date it was published. Students have some difficulty getting used to this, but if you look at an introduction in a journal article, you will find that it is full of citations – between five and ten citations in the first couple of paragraphs is not at all unusual.

Crucial tip	The previous point relates to statements of opinion, as well as statements of psychological fact. If, for example, you write 'a great deal of research has been carried out on...' you should either then list a great deal of research, or say who has made the claim. The same is true for statements like 'most modern psychologists agree that...' or 'little research has been done on...'

You need to state the psychological questions that your research was designed to answer. You will usually have clear hypotheses that you have derived from past research, in which case these can be listed (however, see the next point). Sometimes the purpose of your research is better stated as exploring a variety of factors or answering particular questions. Either way, after reading your introduction someone should have a very clear picture of what you are trying to find out and how it builds on what is already known. Finally, do not state your findings in this section. The introduction should read as though it was written before the research was carried out.

METHOD

This section tells the reader what you actually did. This section should be clear, accurate and complete. Keep in mind while writing it that you are intending to give sufficient information so that a researcher could repeat what you did, *exactly*. The section should be written in the past tense because it is a description of what you did, not a recipe for how to carry out your study. The Method section usually has four distinct subsections, which are described below. You might find in journal articles that they have not always included every subsection, or that they have included an additional section. However, I emphasise again that while a student you should stick to the standard format that I am giving you. One of the purposes of writing a research report is to show your lecturers that you know what a research report should look like. If you change the basic format, it might present your research more clearly, but it will not demonstrate to your lecturers that you know what a research report should look like.

The Method section in your practical reports will probably include more details than those in a journal article. Journal editors prefer to keep Method sections short because they have a limited amount of space available

Design

In the Design section, you outline the structure of your study. The purpose of the design section is to give the reader an overview of the study – if your design was complex, it might be hard for the reader to understand it from a description of what you did. The design section is a little like the ingredients from a recipe – it provides the ingredients of your study which you will use later on in the Method section.

You should state clearly the nature of the research you carried out. Was it an experiment, a correlational study, a case study, etc.? If it was an experiment, did you use a between-participants design (different participants in each condition) or a within-participants design (same participants in each condition) – or was it a mixed design (with both within- and between-participant conditions)? (See Chapter 3.)

Describe the variables that you measured and/or manipulated. If your design was experimental, you should describe the dependent and independent variables. In experimental designs, you should state the number of levels in (each of) the independent variables, and describe them (see Chapter 2).

Describing the dependent variable(s) means actually saying what they are and what they mean. You need to say more than 'the dependent variable was the response the participants gave to the questionnaire'.

Participants

The Participants section is used to briefly describe the makeup of your sample, i.e. the people who took part in your study. You need to tell the reader about your sample so that they can decide whether this was a good enough sample for the purposes of your research. In Chapter 5, we will look at sampling techniques and see some of the things that can go wrong.

Materials

The Materials section (sometimes called Apparatus or Measures) is where you describe anything that you used in the study. This should include technical equipment, questionnaires, word lists, computer programs, etc. It does not need to include pens, paper, tables, or anything extremely obvious. It is very tempting to write the materials section as a list – don't. Always write in full sentences.

Where possible in this section, you should describe accurately the nature of the equipment. Note that some journals recommend that you report the precise model of a piece of equipment (e.g. tape recorder model number ST23451) though usually you can be more easy-going than this – just say you used a tape recorder, and everyone knows what you mean.

You should also include in this section full details of any stimuli used in your study (e.g. word lists, pictures, nonsense syllables, etc.). If the materials, such as a word list, can be described briefly, you should include it here. If it is long, then it should be included as an appendix.

Procedure

In this subsection, you describe precisely what you did while carrying out the study. This section is a full report of what happened, from the selection of the participants to the debriefing.

If your study was an experiment, then you should detail how participants were allocated to the different experimental conditions. If the design was a between-participants design, were participants randomly allocated to the different conditions (and if not why not?)? If the design was a within-participants design, what method of counterbalancing (see Chapter 2) was used and why? Do not simply say 'participants were randomly allocated to one of the conditions'. Instead, describe how you decided which participants were allocated to what part of the experiment.

You should describe the instructions that were presented to participants – don't just say 'participants were given the instructions (see Appendix 2)'. If there were written or standardised instructions then you might want to include them as an appendix. Occasionally the exact wording of instructions is important. If this is the case, you should include the wording in the procedure.

If you debriefed the participants, you should say so.

Crucial tip	Students often lose marks by missing out details in the procedure. It can be useful to pretend that you are trying to repeat the study by carrying out the procedure you have written down – although this is difficult to do because you were there, so you know what happened.

RESULTS

In this section, you report the results of your data analyses. However, you should not discuss or attempt to interpret them in this section. Sometimes you will come across research reports that combine the results and discussion section. Though you might be tempted to do this if you have a large number of results that need to be discussed, it is better to stick to the standard format (for the reasons we have already discussed, more than once).

The first part of the results should say how you calculated the scores for your participants. This will often be obvious; for example, the score might be the number of words correctly remembered. Sometimes the method of scoring will be less obvious, and sometimes it might even be quite complex.

The second part of the results should display descriptive or exploratory statistics (see Chapter 6). The third part of the results should display information about any statistical tests that you carried out.

If you have a number of hypotheses to test, you might prefer to present the descriptive statistics and the inferential statistics together for each hypothesis. Your results section would then look like the following:

> Hypothesis A: descriptive statistics; Hypothesis A: inferential statistics.
>
> Hypothesis B: descriptive statistics; Hypothesis B: inferential statistics.
>
> etc.

It can be difficult to know what level of detail to put in the results section. If what you are putting in this section will help to answer part of your initial questions or hypotheses, then you are right to include it.

The Results section should be easy to understand on its own. Make sure that the reader does not have to keep flicking backwards and forwards to other sections of the report to understand what you are saying. For instance, students sometimes put in the Results section abbreviations that were described in the Materials section. Don't use abbreviations that the reader may not remember.

Crucial tip | Using abbreviations is usually frowned upon. Using abbreviations that are not defined elsewhere is worse. But the most heinous sin is to use variable names from computer output without describing them.

You can report results in many different ways: using a text description, a table or a graph.

For example, you could write 'Group 1 (chocolate) had a mean happiness score of 12.3, higher than group 2 (carrots) whose mean happiness score was 4.1.'

You could present the same information in a table or a graph. Generally, you should choose the method that takes up the least space – but conveys the information clearly. In this example, the text description is acceptable – anyone reading it has all of the information needed– the graph and the table give no new information, and do not enhance our understanding in any way. Choosing the method of presenting the information is, however, a complex issue and is further discussed in Chapter 6.

It is never good enough just to use graphs or tables. You should always have some text that describes what the graph or table shows.

It can be difficult to know how to report statistical tests in text. As a rule, you need to report the test statistic, either the N, or the df (depending on the test) and whether the result is significant. There are two ways of doing this, and either would be appropriate. The first way is just to list the test statistic, the df and the probability: $\chi^2 = 1.3$, $df = 1$, $p > 0.05$. The second way is to put the df (or less commonly the N) in brackets after the test statistic: $t(88) = 2.4$, $p < 0.05$.

If you use a statistical package, it will probably provide you with an exact p value. Rather than just saying $p < 0.05$, it will say $p = 0.023$. Arguments rage in methodological circles about how this should be reported. One side of the argument says that you should simply report whether the result is significant at the 0.05 level or not. So, if the statistics package says that p = 0.0045, you should write p < 0.05. The other side of the argument says that you should write the exact value that is given for p, so if the statistics package says $p = 0.0045$, you write $p = 0.0045$. A sort of compromise is to use cut-off values of 0.05, 0.01 and 0.001. So if the statistics package says that $p = 0.0045$, you should write $p < 0.01$. While many journal articles still use this technique, it is usually frowned upon in methodological circles. I don't know which of these your lecturers will prefer you to use – the best thing for you to do is to find out, and use the same one.

If a statistics package says that $p = 0.000$, it doesn't mean it. It has rounded the value to 3 decimal places, and it means that $p < 0.0005$.

Don't give excessive numbers of decimals. One decimal more than the accuracy of your measure is usually enough. If you measured how many digits people could recall, writing that the mean was 7.1 is fine. Writing that the mean was 7.132384 is far more accuracy than your measure warrants.

DISCUSSION

The discussion section is where you are freed a little from the strict rules about what you should put in your practical report, and you are finally allowed to get a little creative. While this is a good thing in some ways, it also means that you have to think a lot more about what to put in this section.

> Crucial tip   The discussion section can be very difficult to write, and if you leave it to the last minute, you can find that you lack the necessary inspiration and end up with a rather poor (or even non-existent) discussion section.

The discussion falls into three sections:

- What did the study find?
- What do the findings mean?
- What are the implications?

The first section involves a description of your findings – an outline of what was found. This is a summary of the results section, putting an emphasis on answering the questions posed in the introduction. The second section should be a discussion of the possible interpretation of these data, including any flaws in the experimental design or execution which may limit the usefulness of the data.

In the third section of the discussion you should: (a) assess the implications of your study – particularly with regard to any issues that you outlined in your introduction; and (b) consider what questions your research has left unanswered and what new questions it has suggested to you. In this section, you elaborate on the argument you began in your introduction. What this means is that a good discussion depends on having a good introduction. This section should include very little new material or literature.

Do not feel afraid to point out issues that have arisen in your research. No one, ever, has carried out a perfect experiment. Lecturers ask you to carry out practical work so that you learn, so don't be afraid to show that you have learnt from the experience. Sometimes students are afraid to point out possible flaws in their study because they think that lecturers will assume they carried out the research badly, and will therefore give them a lower grade. You can be reassured by two thoughts: first, if there are flaws in your study, your lecturer will notice them whether you point them out or not (they have probably read hundreds of practical reports in the past); second, your lecturers will be happy to see that you have learned from the experience of carrying out the research.

REFERENCING AND REFERENCES

Referencing properly is surprisingly hard work. Your reference section will take a lot longer to write than you imagine. Make sure you find out the guidelines for referencing from your department and follow them.

You should reference all information that you use in your study. And you should include everything in the reference section.

GRAPHS, TABLES AND FIGURES

Label all of your figures, tables and graphs (graphs should also be labelled as figures) using a consecutive numbering scheme that starts with the first one of each to appear in the report (i.e. the first table is Table 1, the first figure or graph is Figure 1, the next table is Table 2 and so on). Then use those labels in your text (e.g. 'as is shown in Figure 1 ...').

All your figures and tables should have detailed, informative titles. Someone should be able to look at a table or a graph and understand it without looking at any of the text.

APPENDICES

While appendices are rare in journal articles because journals don't have the space, your practical report will almost certainly need to have some appendices. Appendices might contain the following:

- *Raw data*. This means a listing of the scores of the participants, which you analysed. It does not mean all of the materials that you collected from the participants. Your lecturers do not want to look through 100 questionnaires which your participants completed. (If you put them in, it also makes the practical reports quite heavy.)
- *Calculations of statistical tests* (if these were done by hand).
- *Informed consent sheet*. If you asked your participants to sign anything to signify that they had given their informed consent to take part in the study, you should include this in the appendix.
- *A copy of any instructions that were used*, which were not given verbatim in the report.
- *Any stimuli that were too large to be included in the materials section of the report*, for example pictures, word lists, questionnaires.

A few additional points

- Don't use sexist language in your report writing. Don't say 'he' when you mean 'he or she' – you might prefer to use 'they' in the singular form (as you read the rest of this book, you will notice that I use this form).
- Personal pronouns (we, I, me) are a very tricky issue. This rule varies between journals, and between departments, but it is *usually* better to avoid using them.

- Remember the person marking the practical. You should always remember that practical reports are marked by your lecturers – who are human beings. Because they are human beings, they will sometimes get annoyed and frustrated by things. Marking practical reports isn't the most interesting thing to do, and so anything you do to make the life of the person marking the report easier may be looked on favourably. (Unfortunately, universities tend to have quite rigorous standards for grading students' work, so by following these rules you will not improve your grade, but your lecturers will like you more.)

  – Unless you are specifically told to, don't put your practical report in hardback ring binder. Your lecturer will probably have many practical reports to mark, and if they are all in ring binders which are very large and heavy, they might make your lecturer unstable on their bicycle.

  – Make sure that the person grading the report can read all of it. If you write or print to the left-hand edge of the page, and then put the report into a binder, your lecturer will not be able to read it. Don't put every page into a separate plastic folder – it takes a long time to take each one out.

  – Use double line spacing.

Finally, read your report and make sure that it is clear and makes sense. If you have the time, you should put it to one side for a little while before you come back to it and read it. If possible, ask a friend to read it – anyone will be able to spot mistakes, and there will almost certainly be some (despite my best efforts, there are almost certainly some in this book).

A note for people who have studied A-level psychology

If you studied A-level psychology, you may feel that you are at a slight advantage over other students. Sometimes this is true, more often it is not. When it comes to report writing, this is definitely not the case. If you had to write reports at A-level, try to erase everything you learned from your brain. The reports that you wrote at A-level will differ in important ways from the reports that you write at degree level, and if you continue to write in the same style, you will lose marks.

Checklist

You can use this checklist as a final examination of your practical report. This is not intended to be an exhaustive set of instructions; rather it contains some of the most common, easily fixed, errors that students make in their reports.

- Is the title short and informative?
- Does the abstract give your conclusions without giving the results of any statistical tests?
- Have you removed all minor details from the abstract?
- Is the abstract 100-150 words and one paragraph long?
- Does the introduction finish with the aim of the research and the hypotheses or predictions that are to be tested?
- Have you described the independent variable and its levels?
- Have you described the dependent variable?
- Have you described your participants in sufficient detail (age, sex)?
- Have you described how your participants were sampled?

- Have you said that you used random sampling? (If you did, you are wrong, so change it.)
- Have you described your materials (not just referred the reader to an appendix)?
- Have you written your materials section as a paragraph?
- Does your procedure contain all the details, which would allow someone else to repeat the experiment? (From when the participant was approached, to when they were debriefed.)
- If your study is an experiment, have you described how you assigned participants to conditions?
- Have you described how your participants were debriefed?
- Have you described how your dependent variable was calculated? (If it was a questionnaire, how was it scored, for example?)
- Have you labelled all graphs and tables clearly (not used abbreviations, and not used variable names from computer printout)?
- Have you used a sensible number of decimal places in your results section?
- Have you reported your statistical tests correctly? Make sure that you have reported the test statistic (F or t, for example), the df or N (and remember that F has two sets of df) and the p value.
- Don't confuse $p < 0.05$ and $p < 0.5$.
- Don't confuse $p < 0.05$ and $p > 0.05$ (the fat end of the arrow points toward the larger number, so $p < 0.05$ means 'p is less than 0.05'.)
- Have you reiterated your results at the start of the discussion?
- Have you referred back to the introduction in your discussion?
- Have you pointed out flaws in your study?
- Have you suggested avenues for future research?
- Have you summarised your findings in your final paragraph?
- Does every reference in your report appear in your references section?
- Do any references appear in your references section, which do not appear in your report?
- Have you put the report in a folder in such a way that all of the text is easily readable?

Further Reading

Many books on research methods have a section that tells you about the structure of psychology practical reports. *Evaluating, Doing and Writing Research in Psychology* by Bell, Staines and Mitchell, goes beyond this, discussing styles of writing and approaches to writing.

The bible of writing research reports is *Publication Manual of the American Psychological Association* (APA; 2001). This has advice on every aspect of research reports you could think of, and a lot that you would never have thought of. The section on referencing describes how to refer to 73 different sources.

Some people recommend the use of a style guide to help you in your writing, such as *The Elements of Style* by Strunk and White (2000). I think it is very difficult to read their advice and then apply it (although you, the reader, might think that I should read it).

CHAPTER I

THE ROLE OF THEORY
IN PSYCHOLOGY

Chapter summary

Studying this Chapter will help you to:

- understand the purpose of scientific research in psychology;
- understand how psychology uses scientific processes to guide research;
- appreciate the role of psychological theory in guiding psychological research.

How will you be assessed on this?

The things you learn in this chapter will be useful for passing this module and also useful for every other module that you do in psychology. Research methods and statistics apply in all areas of psychology.

In practical work

You will be expected to do practical work: to design, carry out, analyse and interpret a piece of psychological research. This book is all about how to do this practical work.

   When you design your research, you need to consider various different approaches you could take to do your study. For example, if you decide to do an experiment, you need to decide upon the appropriate experimental design (see Chapter 2). Then you consider the advantages and disadvantages of each approach, and having done all that, you then use what you believe to be the best. However, in order to achieve higher grades, you have to do more than simply choose the best approach, carry out your study and write up what you did: you also have to justify your choice – make a critical analysis of it by weighing up the advantages and disadvantages of your approach as opposed to other approaches you might have used.

> Crucial tip   Marks are awarded for:
> - doing things as well as possible;
> - understanding that things could have been better.

The information in this chapter will also teach you to evaluate research. Lecturers will ask you to carry out practical work, not only to assess how well you can do it but also to give you practice – you learn by doing. No one expects you to do a perfect piece of research (no one expects *anyone* to do a perfect piece of research). Most researchers look at their finished work and wish that they could go back to the beginning, start again and, this time, avoid all of the mistakes that they made. The same is true for your practical reports. However, it helps to remember that to gain higher grades you do not need to carry out a perfect piece of research (as I said, *nobody* ever does a perfect piece of research), **but** you must show that you are aware of the shortcomings in the research that you did. By being aware of those shortcomings and reflecting on them, you learn to do better next time. Students sometimes notice a flaw in their practical work, but do not point it out for fear that if it is noticed they would get a lower grade. They hope that the marker will not notice the flaw. You can be sure that the person marking the work will notice and will think that *you* were not aware of it. So, for better marks, point out any flaws in your own work, and you will get credit for being able to critically reflect upon your own work. You will show that you have learned from the experience, and that is the point.

> Crucial tip   It is easy to explain what happened when a piece of research is carried out. It is harder to explain (and marks and awarded for) explaining *why* the study was carried out and what the results *mean*.

When you present your own research projects, you will need to explain why you did that piece of research. You did the research to test a theory, and this section examines the links between research and theory.

In essays and exams

You may be examined on the information covered in this chapter. You may be asked multiple choice questions, short answer questions, mini-essays or even full essays, or you may be asked to do a critical evaluation of a research study.

However, even more useful will be the practical use you make of the information when you are doing other psychology modules or courses. In both coursework and exams, higher marks are usually awarded for critical evaluation. Evaluation can be difficult – especially when you come to the part where you have to make positive suggestions as to what the original researcher could have done better. Much of what you learn in this book will be applicable in this way.

Crucial concepts

These are the key terms you will meet in this Chapter:

Alternative hypothesis	Science
Experimental hypothesis	Theory
Hypothesis	Two-tailed hypothesis
Null hypothesis	Variable
One-tailed hypothesis	

Section 1 — How to link theory and research

What are you studying?

This section will look at the relationship between psychological theory and psychological research. We will use some examples of psychological theories to look at the relationship between research and theory.

This section also tells you how to evaluate psychological theory and research. Psychology is a science, and psychological research must be carried out using scientific methods. In this section, we will examine what we mean by science and what we mean when we say that some psychological work is not scientific.

The links between theory and research provide a foundation to much research methodology in psychology. These links might not be taught in your course, and if they are taught, might not be examined. If 'links' are not taught explicitly, or if the subject is not examined, then you may want to skip this section, but I suggest that you do try to understand this chapter because it provides a foundation for the rest of this book.

We start with the description of the role of theories in psychology, and then describe how hypotheses are derived from theories. We then consider a little bit of philosophy of science – how theories and hypotheses relate to one another. Finally, we will look at variables, and see how these relate to theory.

Theories in psychology

In this section, we will examine what makes a good theory and then we will consider why theories are important in psychology.

> Crucial concept *Theories* are used to tie together findings in psychological research.

If there were no theories, then research would consist of disparate findings which bear no relation to one another. If psychologists did not rely upon theories then psychological research would not be able to move forward – it would not be able to link facts together.

We will look at the two roles for theories: the role as glue which holds seemingly isolated findings together and the role as a way of generating new hypotheses which can be tested.

Example: Biological Theory of Extraversion
Consider the finding:

> *When lemon juice is placed on the tongue,*
> *extraverts salivate less than introverts.*

Now we might consider this finding surprising (if you ask most people, they will guess that extraverts would salivate more) but, on its own, at least from the perspective of a psychologist, it is not very interesting. To be interesting to a psychologist, we need to have a theory that explains not only this difference, between introverts and extraverts, but other differences as well. Eysenck (1967) proposed that the difference between introverts and extraverts arises out of a difference in a type of arousal in the nervous system. In other words, the brains of extraverts are less easily aroused than the brains of introverts. Eysenck's theory explains, and brings together, many of the findings on the differences between introverts and extraverts, for example:

- Introverts are more easily conditioned to blink when a buzzer sounds.

- Introverts and extraverts differ in their reaction to both sedative drugs and stimulant drugs.

- Introverts are better at vigilance tasks (tasks that involve looking out for something).

Eysenck's theory tied all these *findings* together by providing an explanation. This explanation also explained a large number of observed differences between introverts and extraverts. If the brain of an introvert is easily aroused, they will find reading a book is enough to keep them occupied; however, the brain of an extravert will not find reading a book to be interesting. Similarly, for music to penetrate the under-aroused brain of the extravert, it might have to be loud; but the introvert, whose brain is more sensitive, may enjoy music that is played softly.

The theory also has *implications*. An extravert will not perform well in a job that requires long periods of concentration looking for a rare signal – their brain would switch off. An extravert would make a poor proofreader, whose job is to read books (such as this one) before they are printed to search for mistakes – the job would not be stimulating enough, and their brain would, effectively, switch off.

This theory invites us to make further hypotheses that can be tested, for example that there is some fairly fundamental biological difference between introverts and extraverts. We can test our further hypotheses by looking for these differences, for instance by using an electroencephalograph (EEG) to study the differences in brain activity. Gale (1973) reviewed a number of EEG studies and found notable differences between introverts and extraverts. A second hypothesis is that if the degree of extraversion is related to some biological difference we should find that it is an inherited trait and not the result of environmental factors. Loehlin (1992) reviewed a large number of studies looking at the heritability of extraversion, and concluded that there are strong genetic influences on the trait of extraversion.

Section summary

Theories are very important in psychological research. A good theory should do three things: it should explain findings; it should have implications; and it should generate further testable hypotheses. Theories serve the function of binding together knowledge, and providing a framework upon which more knowledge can be built.

Section 2	Testing theories: hypotheses

What are you studying?

In the last section we looked at psychological theories, and talked about how theories generate hypotheses. In this section we will have a closer look at hypotheses, and consider how a theory modifies a hypothesis.

What are hypotheses?

> Crucial concept A *hypothesis* (plural hypotheses) is a testable statement, derived from a theory, which is used to test that theory.

To understand the relationship between theories and hypotheses we need first to consider what we mean by science. Science as a whole is not necessarily about test tubes, chemicals, smells or electronics.

> Crucial concept *Science* is about an approach to research. Psychology is a science and uses a scientific approach.

(It is interesting to note that sometimes students of subjects such as biology, chemistry or physics may consider that psychology is not a science, but often do not know what it is that makes a science into a science.[1])

Instead of thinking about any difficult, abstract psychological theories, let's think about a theory we are all pretty familiar with – let us consider the theory of gravity. An apple fell from a tree and landed on Isaac Newton's head, or so the story goes. He wondered why the apple fell, and decided to make up a theory to explain it. He called his theory the Theory of Gravity. As we said before, a good theory should explain what happened, make further predictions and have implications. The Theory of Gravity says (roughly) that there is an attractive force between objects that is dependent on the mass of the objects. The earth, of course, has a large mass and is therefore extremely attractive to objects – therefore *things tend to fall towards the ground*. The Theory of Gravity explains why the apple fell, makes a large number of further predictions (a theory of gravity that applied only to apples would not be a very good theory) and has a very large number of implications – for instance, about the movement of heavenly bodies such as the planets and the sun.

---

[1] Although if you are a student of biology, chemistry or physics please accept my apologies.

Testing theories by testing hypotheses

> Crucial concept   A *hypothesis* is a testable statement derived from a theory. A hypothesis is a statement that predicts what will happen.

Hypotheses (usually) come in two flavours. These are the *null hypothesis* and the *alternative hypothesis* (sometimes called the *experimental hypothesis*). They are sometimes written as H_0 (the null hypothesis) and H_1 (the alternative hypothesis).

> Crucial concept   The *experimental hypothesis* (sometimes the *alternative hypothesis*), or H_1, is a statement made by your theory.

Suppose your theory says that all swans are white. The alternative hypothesis H_1 will state: 'There are no black swans.'

> Crucial concept   The *null hypothesis*, H_0, is the negation of your theory.

The null hypothesis, H_0, will state the opposite: 'There is at least one black swan.'[2]

In this case, the theory and the hypothesis are very similar. There is really only one hypothesis that can be derived from the theory. Usually there are many hypotheses that can be derived from the theory.

If we have another look at the theory of extraversion that we covered earlier (if you have jumped in at this point, you might want to go and have a quick read of that section), we can derive more hypotheses from these two theories. The biological theory of extraversion states: 'Introverts are more easily aroused than extraverts.' We can generate other hypotheses from this theory, and for each hypothesis we can generate a corresponding null hypothesis.

For example, we might hypothesise that extraverts have a higher pain threshold than introverts:

H_1: Extraverts have a higher pain threshold than introverts.

H_0: Extraverts do *not* have a higher pain threshold than introverts.

We could hypothesise that extraverts will wake up more slowly than introverts:

H_1: Extraverts are less aroused 10 minutes after waking than introverts.

H_0: Extraverts are *not* less aroused 10 minutes after waking than introverts.

THE IMPORTANCE OF THE NULL HYPOTHESIS

At this point, you might be asking why we seem to be so interested in the null hypothesis. Surely the alternative hypothesis, the one that is proposed by our theory, is more important?

Well, yes it is. However, we can never prove the alternative hypothesis. What we do instead is see if we can disprove, or reject, the null hypothesis. If we can't reject the null hypothesis, this doesn't really mean that our alternative hypothesis is correct – our alternative hypothesis was a bit vague anyway – but it does provide support for our alternative hypothesis. Because of

---

[2] To make things easier, we are pretending that there are only two possible types of swans – black and white.

this, this approach is sometimes called 'the method of indirect support'.

In psychology, we can't usually make definite statements about the null hypothesis. We collect data to test the null hypothesis, and it is the results of the analysis of these data that we can talk about rather than the null hypothesis itself.

We say that it is either likely or unlikely that we would have found these results were the null hypothesis to be true.

According to the results of our study, we make one of two statements, we either '*reject the null hypothesis*', or we '*fail to reject the null hypothesis*'.

Note that these two statements can be written in many different ways, but we should always talk in terms of either rejecting or not rejecting the null hypothesis. Some versions that you might come across (or be tempted to write) are shown in the table below. Although they all look equivalent, you should only use the first version.

	Theory supported	Theory not supported
✓	Reject H_0	Fail to reject H_0
✗	Accept H_1	Accept H_0
✗	Fail to reject H_1	Fail to accept H_1
✗	Fail to accept H_0	Reject H_1

ONE-TAILED AND TWO-TAILED HYPOTHESES

Hypotheses come in two kinds: one-tailed and two-tailed hypotheses.

A two-tailed hypothesis states that there will be a difference between two (or more) measures, or a relationship between two (or more) measures. An example of a two-tailed hypothesis is that 'Introverts and extraverts will differ in the amount of saliva they produce when lemon juice is placed on their tongue.'

> Crucial concept A *one-tailed hypothesis* states that there will be an effect, and that it will go in a particular direction.

An example of a one-tailed hypothesis is: 'Introverts will salivate more than extraverts when lemon juice is placed on their tongue.' A one-tailed hypothesis is sometimes called a directional hypothesis (because it states a direction for the effect) (see Figure 1.1).

> Crucial concept A *two-tailed hypothesis* states that there will be an effect, but does not state the direction of the effect.

An example of a two-tailed hypothesis is: 'There will be a difference in the amount of saliva produced by introverts and extraverts when lemon juice in placed on their tongue.' A two-tailed hypothesis is sometimes called a 'non-directional' hypothesis because it specifies that there is an effect, but doesn't specify a direction for that effect (see Figure 1.2).

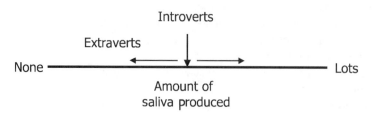

Figure 1.1: A directional (one-tailed) hypothesis. The hypothesis says that extraverts will be different from introverts (just like the one-tailed hypothesis), but that the difference will be in one direction only.

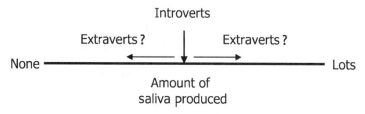

Figure 1.2: A non-directional (two-tailed) hypothesis. The hypothesis says that the extraverts will be different from the introverts, but the extraverts could be on either side.

Crucial tip   Make sure that your alternative hypothesis (H_1) and your null hypothesis (H_0) are both of the same form. For example:

H_1: Extraverts will salivate less than introverts when lemon juice is placed on their tongue.
H_0: There will be no difference between the amount of saliva produced by introverts and extraverts when lemon juice is placed on their tongue.
H_1 is a one-tailed (directional) alternative hypothesis. H_0 is a two-tailed (non-directional) null hypothesis. This is wrong.

All hypotheses talk about variables. When a hypothesis mentions a variable, it mentions it in an abstract, psychological way. We need to move from the abstract, psychological representation to a more concrete representation – this is known as *operationalising* the variables. We will have a look at what we mean by this by looking at a study that is examining the effects of a depressant drug on complex skill performance.

Variables

Crucial concept   A *variable* is something that can change (or vary) between people.

Hypotheses propose that there will be a relationship between two (or more) variables, and every study in psychology involves at least one, and usually more than one, variable.

We will use the example of a psychologist who has a theory about the effects of depressant drug consumption on complex motor skill performance. They devise an experimental hypothesis: 'Depressant drugs will affect complex skill performance.'

There are two variables, depressant drug consumption and complex motor skill performance, and we are interested in their relationship.

This theory is interested in complex skill performance, but we can think of many different complex skills that we could assess. In Figure 1.3 we have a circle labelled 'Complex motor skill'. The theory talks about 'complex skill performance' and so we will label this as the theoretical level of the variable.

'Complex motor skill' is a rather vague, fluffy name for a variable. We need to make it a little more concrete – we need to *conceptualise* complex motor skill performance. The next stage is to decide what sort of complex motor skill we will measure. There are many ways that we could conceptualise complex motor skill: walking, driving, throwing darts at a dartboard, throwing balls of paper at a waste paper bin, typing. We need to decide which of these methods we will use. When we have decided, we have defined the variable at the conceptual level. The psychologist, as you can see in Figure 1.3 decides to conceptualise complex motor skill as 'walking'.

Therefore, the psychologist has decided to measure 'walking', but this could be done in many ways. How will we actually measure the variable 'walking'? What operations will we perform to measure this? Because we are now talking in terms of the operations that we will use, we are *operationalising* the variable. We can operationalise the measurement of walking in many ways, for example:

- Time taken to walk 5 metres.
- Number of times participant falls off stepping stones while crossing river.
- Number of times participant steps off a straight line.

Each of these would be a different (and equally legitimate) operationalisation of the conceptual variable 'walking'.

This whole process of moving from a theoretical variable, to a conceptual variable to an operational variable is shown in Figure 1.3.

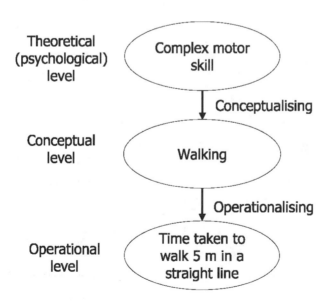

Figure 1.3: Operationalising the variables.

> Crucial tip
>
> When you are describing a variable, you need to describe it at each of the levels. It is no good saying 'Participants filled in the following questionnaire' without saying what the questionnaire was measuring. Similarly, it is no good to say 'We measured participants' attitudes towards hospital food' without saying how you measured the attitudes.

Section summary

There are hypotheses: the experimental (or alternative) hypothesis H_1 and the null hypothesis H_0. It is the null hypothesis that is tested. If the null hypothesis is rejected, this provides indirect support for the experimental hypothesis.

There are two types of hypothesis: a one-tailed hypothesis predicts that there will be an effect and specifies the direction of the effect; a two-tailed hypothesis specifies that there will be an effect but does not specify the direction of that effect.

Theories and hypotheses make mention of variables, but there are many different ways of conceptualising and operationalising a variable — you need to make it clear in your practical reports how you did this.

Section 3   Putting it all together

What are you studying?

In this section we will look at how all of the things we have said about theories, hypotheses and variables link together.

Figure 1.4 shows a diagrammatic representation of the theory testing process. At the top is the theoretical level — when we start we have a theory. We want to test the theory, but a theory is a very big thing to test in one go, so instead of testing the theory, we test a hypothesis derived from that theory. In the example we used in the last section we had a theory that 'Depressant drugs affect motor skill performance.'

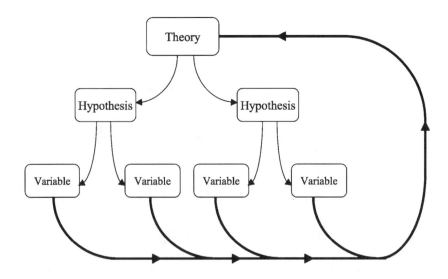

Figure 1.4: Diagram of the theory testing/modification process.

For any theory, there are many hypotheses that can be tested. A hypothesis is a statement about the relations between the variables. For every hypothesis, especially in psychology, there are many ways of defining and measuring the variables which are mentioned in the hypothesis.

The hypotheses which are tested either provide support for the theory, or they disprove the theory. (Remember the theory cannot be proved, only supported.) If the theory is wrong, it needs to be either rejected completely or modified. The support or modification of the theory is represented by the arrow showing the hypothesis feeding back to the theory.

Methods used in psychology

The null hypothesis testing method is now the main method that is used in psychology; however, the use of this method is comparatively recent. Can you think of any studies or theories that did not use the null hypothesis testing method, and may have been improved if they had used this method?

Answer

There are many theories from the history of psychology where people tried to prove that their theories were correct instead of trying to prove that their theories were wrong. We will consider some examples that you may have encountered already in your studies. If you are unfamiliar with these studies, you will find them in any introductory psychology textbook.

Piaget's studies of cognitive development in children

Jean Piaget was a Swiss psychologist who studied the development of thinking in children. He suggested that children were able to carry out certain cognitive tasks only after they reached certain ages. In particular, he thought that children below the age of about 7 were unable to think about abstract things (things which are not here and now). He showed to his own satisfaction that children under 7 were incapable of certain tasks.

However, more recent studies have found that children are more capable of abstract thought than was previously considered possible. Piaget was trying to show that children could not do something, and so designed experiments to demonstrate how incapable they were. He was using the inductive method, finding one example after another of children being incapable of doing particular tasks. More recent experiments were designed to try to find out just what children could do; they tried to show that Piaget's theory was wrong (or at least that it was in need of modification), and these experimenters managed to find some circumstances in which children could be persuaded to think about abstract things. They used the null hypothesis testing method to find some evidence that could not be accounted for by the theory.

Freud's theories of personality and psychopathology

In the later nineteenth century and first half of the twentieth century Sigmund Freud developed a theory of personality and psychopathology. He developed his ideas from the information patients gave him in therapy sessions. Freud attempted to develop a theory that could explain why the patients had the thoughts and feelings that they did. However, he did not develop this theory in such a way that it gave rise to testable hypotheses. This means that it is difficult (or impossible) to prove that the theory is untrue. For example, one of Freud's theories suggests that if your father behaved in an oppressive manner towards you, you might respond by identifying with your father and therefore loving him. The theory also suggests that, on the other hand, you might end up hating him. Freud's theory can explain any result, love or hate, and so either outcome is explained by his theory and no outcome disproves it. The hypothetico-deductive method requires a statement which is testable — one outcome supports it, another outcome disproves it. In fact, it is very difficult to apply the null hypothesis testing method to Freud's theory, because Freud's theory does not give rise to testable hypotheses.[3]

Section summary

A theory is used to develop hypotheses. Each hypotheses can be operationalised in many different ways using different variables. The hypotheses are then tested and used to modify the theory. This cycle of testing and modifying theories is known as the hypothetico-deductive method.

Further reading

Patrick McGhee's book *Thinking Psychologically* (Basingstoke: Palgrave, 2001) is a good introduction to ways of thinking about different types of research, and explores some alternative approaches to psychological research.

A book which covers lots of useful material for thinking about why we do psychological research is *Evaluating, Doing and Writing Research in Psychology* by Bell, Staines and Mitchell (published by Sage).

Also recommended is Chapter 1 of *Understanding Psychological Science* by Jones (published by HarperCollins).

[3] Some researchers, notably Kline (1981) and Eysenck (1985), have attempted to derive testable hypotheses from Freud's theory, and generally find that the theory does not make accurate predictions.

CHAPTER 2

COLLECTING DATA –
EXPERIMENTAL DESIGN

Chapter summary

Studying this Chapter will help you to:

- Understand the basics of experimental design and the structure of experiments.
- Identify the independent and dependent variable in an experiment.
- Evaluate an experiment in terms of the design and setting.

How will you be assessed on this?

You are likely to be tested on your knowledge of experiments in two different ways:

- As part of your practical work you will need to know how to design experiments and carry them out, and you will need to know the correct terminology to describe the experiments.

- As well as doing your own experiments, you might be asked to read about experiments that have been carried out and then make a critical evaluation of those experiments. Of course, to know what a researcher might have done well or done wrong, you need to know how things should be done properly.

Crucial concepts

These are the key terms you will meet in this Chapter:

Bias	Laboratory study
Confound	Levels of independent variables
Counterbalancing	Participant effects
Dependent variable (DV)	Random assignment
Experiment	Random effects
Experimenter effects	Randomisation
Extraneous variables	Repeated measures design
Field study	Situation variables
Independent groups design	Systematic effects
Independent variable (IV)	

Section I   The structure of experiments

What are you studying?

This section briefly introduces the idea of an experiment and explains what makes experiments different from other research techniques. We introduce some of the important aspects of experiments.

What is an experiment?

In layperson's terms, an experiment is an attempt to find something out or to investigate something. In psychology, the word experiment has a more specific meaning, and when you are doing psychology, you should make sure that you use the word in its correct, technical sense.

> Crucial concept   An *experiment* is carried out to test a hypothesis, by manipulating one or more variable(s) and measuring one or more variable(s).

In psychology, a hypothesis is a statement usually in the form 'X affects Y'. Does X indeed affect Y? Suppose our hypothesis is 'Noise affects ability to carry out a mathematical task.' How do we find out? We ask people to do mathematical tasks. We inflict noise on them while they are doing the tasks. We get the test results and analyse under what noise conditions the results were good and under what conditions the results were not so good.

> Crucial concept The *independent variable* (often abbreviated to *IV*) is the variable that we manipulate.

In the example above, the independent variable is *noise*.

> Crucial concept The *dependent variable* (often abbreviated to *DV*) is the variable that we measure.

In the example above, the dependent variable is the success our subjects have in doing the mathematical task – their *test scores*. Our alternative (experimental) hypothesis states that by changing the IV (noise), we will have an effect on the DV (results of the maths tests). The structure of a simple experiment is shown in Figure 2.1.

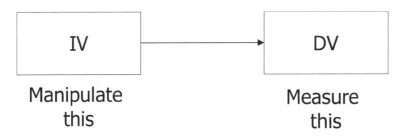

Figure 2.1: The relationship between the independent variable and the dependent variable.

> Crucial tip It is in experiments, and only in experiments, that we manipulate an independent variable and measure a dependent variable. If you (or someone else) did not manipulate an independent variable and measure a dependent variable, they did not do an experiment.

However, the independent variable (in our experiment, the noise) is not the only thing that influences the dependent variable (in our experiments, the maths test results).

> Crucial concept *Extraneous variables* are additional variables that influence the dependent variable.

There are two kinds of extraneous variables, and they each have a different sort of influence on the results. Extraneous variables can have *random* effects and *systematic* effects.

> Crucial concept *Random* effects have an effect on all participants, but not in a predictable way.

If there is a random effect in an experiment, it means that some people's scores on the DV will be lowered and some people's scores on the DV will be raised, but the average effect is zero – the effects cancel each other out. The most common random effect that we have to deal with is individual differences – everyone has different abilities at maths. Random extraneous variables are troublesome, but we can live with them if we can minimise their effects.

> Crucial concept   *Systematic effects* (sometimes known as *biases*) have an effect on some participants more than others and will bias the results of an experiment.

A variable that causes a systematic effect is called a *confounding variable* (or sometimes just a confound) or bias. A confound, bias or systematic effect is not randomly distributed; rather it affects some group(s) more than other group(s). Because systematic effects influence one group more than they influence others, it will disguise the effect of the independent variable. In the example above, if we allowed the 'silent' group more time to do the maths test than the 'noise' group, we could not be sure that any differences between the groups were due to the independent variable – they might be due to a systematic extraneous variable.

Let's summarise what we have been saying and examine the experiment that we have been describing in a little more detail. Here is the method we used in the experiment to test the hypothesis that noise influences maths test results. Twenty participants were randomly divided into two groups of ten, and each participant was given ten maths problems to solve in ten minutes. The first group were asked to do the problems in quiet conditions, the second were placed in an identical room, and asked to do the problems while four radios were playing at the same time, each one on a different station.

Of course, because of random extraneous variables, we expect people to get a range of different scores, but we expect that *on average* the quiet group will get higher scores than the noise group. (If there were no random extraneous variables, the quiet group would all get the same score, which would be higher than the score for the noise group.)

Much more serious than the effect produced by the random extraneous variables discussed above are the bias effects resulting from a systematic extraneous variable (or confound). It can be hard work to randomly assign participants to conditions, so instead of using *random* assignment, we assign people to one group or the other in the order in which they turn up for the experiment. The first ten people will be assigned to the Quiet condition, the second ten people will be assigned to the Noise condition. This method is, after all, much easier than assigning people randomly, and surely it will make no difference?

First, yes this method is much easier. Second, this lazy method might well make a difference to our results. Why should it make a difference? To see why, we have to consider why some of the people turned up later than other people. Are there *really* no differences between people who arrive on time and the people who arrive late? It might be that the people who arrive late are generally less conscientious about many things. The people who arrived late maybe were late in getting up because they went out last night and so they are tired, possibly hung over, they may not have had breakfast or brushed their teeth, and will generally be feeling worse. It might be the people who arrived late had been at a special class for high achievers in mathematics that was in the other building, or it could be that they had been attending an additional lecture designed for students with hearing difficulties. The trouble is, we do not know the reason for their lateness, and if we don't know the reason, we cannot rely on the late people being the same, for our purposes, as the early people.

Simpson's paradox (Simpson, 1951) is a nice example, which shows the importance of random assignment of participants to conditions, and we explore this below.

'Simpson's Paradox' and random assignment

Simpson's paradox is an interesting puzzle in methodology which shows the importance of random assignment of participants to conditions. The hypothetical experiment below shows Simpson's paradox in action.

This example, from Pearl (2000), gives the results of a simple experiment to examine whether taking a headache pill reduces a headache and are shown in the table below. It shows that one group of 40 participants took a pill for their headache and of those 40 people 50% have been cured. A second group of 40 participants took no pill for their headache, and we find that only 40% of these people have been cured. It seems clear from this that we would suggest that taking a pill is likely to cure your headache.

All participants

	Headache gone	Headache not gone	% cured
Pill	20	20	50
No pill	16	24	40

But the researchers who carried out the experiment did not randomly assign people to the two conditions.

When they did the analysis with males only, they found the results shown in the table below. So, for the males, the drug did not seem to work – 70% of those who did not take the pill were cured and only 60% of those who did take the pill were cured.

Males only

	Headache gone	Headache not gone	% cured
Pill	18	12	60
No pill	7	3	70

'OK,' said the researchers, 'it doesn't work for men, it just works for women.' So, as a double check, they did the analysis on the women only. The results are shown in the table below, and as you can see, of the women who took the pill, 20% were cured, whereas of the women who didn't take the pill 30% were cured.

Females only

	Headache gone	Headache not gone	% cured
Pill	2	8	20
No pill	9	21	30

This seems to be impossible! The pill works for 'people', yet it doesn't work for men, nor does it work for women. So what is going on? The answer is that the researchers did not randomly assign participants to conditions. A higher proportion of men decided to take the pill (30 out of 40 men decided to take the pill), only a small proportion of women decided to take the pill (10 out of 40 women decided to take the pill). And men were more likely to get better, whether they took a pill or not.

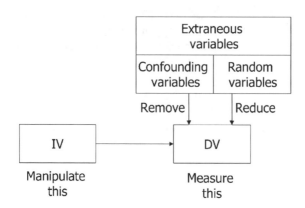

Figure 2.2: The relationship between the IV and the DV, including extraneous variables.

A summary of the experimental design process is shown in Figure 2.2. The independent variable (which we manipulate) affects the dependent variable (which we measure). Extraneous variables also affect the dependent variable. We should attempt to remove all confounding variables (biases), and to minimise the effects of random variables. In the following sections, we will have a closer look at each of the types of variables (independent, dependent and extraneous), and consider some of the choices that you have to make when you are designing and carrying out experiments.

Section summary

This section has introduced the important features of experiments that we will look at in more detail in the rest of the chapter. Experiments feature an independent variable (IV) which is manipulated by the experimenter, and a dependent variable (DV) which is measured by the experimenter. Extraneous variables also affect the DV, and we aim to remove, or minimise, their effect. One of the most important aspects of experimental design is random assignment of different participants to different conditions – if you do not randomly assign participants to conditions, you cannot be sure that any differences in the conditions are due to the independent variable.

Section 2 Independent variables

What are you studying?

In this section we will look at some of the different ways in which independent variables (IVs) can be operationalised. We will focus on mood as an independent variable that can be operationalised in many different ways.

An independent variable in an experiment is one that is manipulated by the experimenter. The manipulation is carried out to determine the effect this variable has on the dependent variables. It is *independent* because it is manipulated *independently* from any changes in other variables. The independent variable is the *cause* of something and the dependent variable is the effect.

As we saw in Chapter 2, the independent variable will be specified by our theory, but the theory will talk about the variable in psychological terms. The theory will use words like 'noise' or 'learning' or 'scores on a maths test'. We need to make those psychological terms real. We need to specify what we will do, to make those psychological terms real – we need to say what operations we will carry out when we do this. Because we need to specify the operations that we will carry out, this process is sometimes called *operationalising*. A definition that tells you what the process was is called an *operational definition*.

We can operationalise independent variables in very many ways, and a different approach might have different implications.

- When you are designing a study, you need to consider the different ways in which you could operationalise the independent variable.
- When you are reading about a study, you must consider whether they have operationalised the independent variable in the best way, or whether, if the researchers had done it differently, they would have had a different result.

Any independent variable can be operationalised in many ways. We will consider one independent variable – mood – in some detail, and look at some different ways in which it could be operationalised. It is possible to go through a similar process for almost every independent variable.

Psychologists are often interested in the effects of mood on different tasks. To experimentally investigate what effect mood has, we need to be able to change people's moods. Usually we want to make one group of people happy and one group sad.

There are many ways of inducing different moods in participants (for a review, see Gerrards-Hesse, Spies and Hesse, 1994). Some of them include the following:

- Weather – wait until a rainy day for sad participants, wait until a sunny day for happy participants. (Or as Rind, 1996, did, put participants in a position where they cannot see the weather, and then tell them that it is raining, or sunny.)
- Gifts – give participants a gift to make them happy. Sweets which remind them of childhood can work well – Love Hearts, for example. (You might be aware that Love Hearts have recently been updated, and included requests such as 'Email me'. These usually raise a smile, which is what we want.)
- False feedback – ask people to fill out a questionnaire (intelligence or personality) and then provide false feedback about the results. ('You have done less well than average on this test. Do you usually find tests difficult?' or 'The test suggests that you may have some insecurities. Do you have problems making friends?')
- Music – play happy music (for example, the Beatles: 'Yellow Submarine') or play sad music for example, Prokofiev: 'Russia under the Mongolian yoke' at half speed.)
- Give people a drug that will induce the appropriate mood.

Each of these methods of mood induction would be appropriate for the hypothesis we wish to test, and each would be likely to give slightly different results, although each is a perfectly valid representation of the independent variable that we are interested in.

Crucial tip	In a psychology experiment, we want to create in the participant a particular psychological state. We are not interested in the independent variable for itself – we are interested in the psychological state created by the independent variable, and it is important to distinguish between these two things.

For example, a psychologist who is interested in stereotyping introduces two people to a group. The psychologist tells the groups that one person is from Queens, New York, and the other is from Manhattan, New York. The psychologist is not interested in Queens and Manhattan, they are interested in the psychological states that are induced by the beliefs. However, if you replicate this study in the UK, it will make no sense, because Queen's and Manhattan, New York, don't mean anything to people in the UK. You should always consider whether the IV is appropriate for the cultural group that you are studying, and the historical period that you are in.

Levels of independent variables

IVs are usually described as having levels. If your experiment comprises one IV which has two forms, it is described as having two levels. Examples of this would be noise and no noise, or happy mood and sad mood.

Sometimes one of those conditions can be considered a neutral condition, in which case the group that is experiencing that neutral condition would be called the *control* group, while the group experiencing one of the other conditions would be an *experimental* group. Thus in the example we considered earlier on in this chapter, the *noise* group would be considered to be the experimental group, and the *no noise* group would be considered to be the control group.

Note: The above is a second meaning of the word 'control.' We also use 'control' to mean ways of controlling extraneous variables.

In some experiments, there may be more than two groups. We might have a no-noise experimental condition and the group tested in this condition would be considered the control group. There might also be a quiet noise condition and a loud noise condition and the two groups experiencing these respective noise conditions would be called the experimental groups. So there would be two experimental groups and one control group.

A further complication is that there may be more than one IV. We might have three noise groups (none, quiet, loud) combined with two mood groups (happy, sad). In effect, we then have six groups. In this case, we would probably not talk of a control group. This experiment would be described as a 3 × 2 design (spoken as 'three by two') (see Figure 2.3).

		IV 1 (Noise)		
		Silent	Quiet	Loud
IV 2 (Mood)	Happy	1	2	3
	Sad	4	5	6

Figure 2.3: A 3 × 2 design, incorporating two independent variables, noise (which has three levels) and mood (which has two levels)

Section summary

This section has focused on operationalising independent variables – that is turning the variable from a psychological concept into a physical reality. We looked at noise and mood as examples of variables that can be defined in many different ways. Finally, we looked at levels of independent variable and at some occasions where there may be more than two levels of the independent variable.

Section 3   Dependent variables

What are you studying?

In an experiment, the experimenter measures the dependent variable. In this section we will look briefly at dependent variables; however, we cover measurement in much more detail in Chapter 5.

The dependent variable (DV) in an experiment is the variable that the experimenter measures to see what the effect was of the independent variable. It is *dependent* because it depends on (we hope) the independent variable. As with IVs, there is a great deal of choice about how you go about operationalising the DV. We will consider the operationalisation and measurement of dependent variables in much more detail in Chapter 5; however, in this section we will have a quick look at some of the decisions that need to be made.

We will use the example of the measurement of driving ability. If we are interested in using driving ability as a DV in an experiment (in other words, find out what affects driving ability), we have a very large choice of things that we could measure. Here are some ways we could do it.

1. Ask someone to drive around a car park, avoiding obstacles. (But how much do we penalise them for hitting an obstacle?)

2. Ask someone to negotiate obstacles in a car park in reverse.

3. Ask someone to drive around a course as quickly as possible.

4. Test someone's simple reaction time. (Stimulus appears, press a button.)

5. Test someone's choice reaction time. (Stimulus appears: if the stimulus is red, press the right button; if green, press the left button.)

6. Test ability to recognise road signs.

7. Test ability to make perceptual judgements of speed of cars.

8. Test ability to make judgements of stopping distances of cars.

9. Ask questions on the Highway Code.

10. Use a driving simulator machine to test speed of reaction to objects in the road.

Each of these tests is different, and may lead to a different assessment of ability, but each of them is one possible measure of driving ability. There are many ways of measuring dependent variables, but (usually) they can be broadly broken down into three different types: verbal measures, behavioural measures and physiological measures, and we will discuss these in Chapter 5.

Section summary

This section has briefly examined the different ways in which dependent variables can be operationalised. We said that there were many different ways of operationalising different dependent variables, just as there were many ways of operationalising independent variables. We look much more closely at measurement in Chapter 5.

Section 4   Extraneous variables

The third type of variable that we need to consider are extraneous variables. These are variables that affect the dependent variable, along with the independent variable. If we want to get accurate and 'true' results from our experiments we need to try to remove or minimise the effects of extraneous variables. When you read about other people's research, you should see if you think that there are any uncontrolled extraneous variables in their research.

The third type of variable is the trickiest for you to deal with, and this type is a pain for other researchers – these are the extraneous variables. Extraneous variables are additional variables, which, along with the IV, affect the DV. When you design studies, you always need to try to take extraneous variables into account, and either minimise them or remove them.

Removing the effect of extraneous variables is called *controlling*, and the specific steps you take are known as *controls*. (Note that this is a second use of the word 'control', different from the 'control group'.)

If there are extraneous variables which you have specifically dealt with and which you have ensured will not have any effect, then these variables are referred to as *controlled variables*.

In addition, when you read about studies, you should try to determine whether there were any uncontrolled extraneous variables not accounted for.

As we saw earlier in this chapter, extraneous variables can have two types of effect: *random* and *systematic*.

Random extraneous variables affect all your participants randomly – each person's score on a dependent variable will be increased or decreased a little because of this, but on average the effects cancel each other out and are therefore not all that problematic. Random extraneous variables increase the amount of variation and obscure the effect of the independent variable, so we would like to reduce them as much as possible. However, we cannot hope to eliminate random extraneous variables.

Systematic extraneous variables are much more of a headache. A systematic extraneous variable affects one level of the IV, but does not affect the other level. If we find a difference between our two (or more) groups in an experiment, we cannot be sure that the differences were not due to extraneous variables. Similarly, if we do not find any difference, it may be that there would have been a difference, but the extraneous variables have obscured its effect.

In this section, we will consider the different types of extraneous variables and look at some of the ways that extraneous variables can be controlled. We will look at four types of extraneous variables: situation variables, participant variables, participant effects and experimenter effects.

Situation variables

Crucial concept   *Situation variables* are anything about the situation which may affect the performance of your participants.

Situation variables are dangerous because if you are not careful they will exert a systematic effect on your dependent variable.

If you are carrying out an experiment in which you decide to give two groups of participants a memory test, you have several options about how to test these two groups, some of which are as follows:

1. Ask everyone to arrive at the same time. Test one group first, and then, when you have finished, test the second group.

2. Ask one group to come in the morning and one group to come in the afternoon.

3. Ask both groups to come at the same time, on different days.

4. Test both groups on the same day, at the same time, in different rooms.

What would you do? Decide, before you read on. Below, we will identify some of the problems associated with each of those methods.

1. If you ask all of your participants to arrive at the same time, one group will have to sit around and get bored while the other group does the task. Because that group has been sitting around getting bored, the groups will no longer be similar, you will have the 'fresh' group and the 'bored' group.

2. If you test people on the same day, the time that you test them may have an effect. If you test both groups in the morning, the earlier group may be more tired, and the later group (as lunchtime approaches) may be hungry. If you test in the afternoon, the first group may be suffering from a drop in arousal as they digest their food. If you test them at the end of the day, the second group may be lethargic and wanting to go home.

3. You could test both groups on different days at the same time – this would avoid the problems that we identified above. However, here you may encounter a systematic variable that is something to do with the day of the week. When I started lecturing there was a popular student night on Tuesdays. The lecture on Wednesday morning had fewer people in it than on other days, and those attending were noticeably less enthusiastic than usual.

4. Testing in different rooms solves some of the problems that we identified above. However, the rooms may differ in size, atmosphere, temperature, lighting and other environmental variables, and any of these might have an effect on results. Moreover, you may have to use different experimenters who may have a different effect on the way the participants react. (Although this effect is less likely to be a problem in this type of cognitive psychology experiment.)

OK, let's stop being so negative and have a look at what we can actually do.

One approach is to test everyone in the same place at the same time. To do this, you have to have some method of presenting the material individually. You might give out written materials or present spoken materials through headphones. However, testing everyone at the same time might be difficult or in some cases impossible.

A different approach is to try to cancel out the effects of any extraneous variables or to ensure that any effects are consistent across groups. This ensures that they will not have a biasing effect on the experiment. Thus, if you have two experimenters, you could arrange that each experimenter could run half of each group. Or, half of each group could be tested in the morning, and half in the afternoon. Or half of each group can be tested in one room, and the other half in a different room. By splitting the groups in this way you can ensure that, if the extraneous variables that we mentioned do have a systematic effect, they would have an equal effect on each condition.

Participant variables

Everybody is different.[1]

If you want to carry out research using 'a person' or 'an adolescent' or 'a 45-year-old female' or 'a student' or 'a person who has been diagnosed with autism', you cannot simply go and find one of these people – because every person that you choose may be different from all of the other people in that category.

This leads to two issues. The first is that we must select a large enough group of participants, and we must select them in an appropriate fashion, to ensure that they are representative of all the people that we are interested in – this issue we will deal with in Chapter 5. Second, the fact that people are different means that we have an additional extraneous variable – a participant variable. The effect of this extraneous variable may be either systematic or random. We must try to ensure that the effect is random rather than systematic (this is very important), and we must try to ensure that the effect of the extraneous variable is as low as possible. We will look at three ways of dealing with, or controlling, this extraneous variable.

The first method is not to study two groups of people at all, but rather to study the same people twice – doing this is called a *repeated measures* design. We discuss the pros and cons of this design later on in this chapter.

The second method you might use is to create two matched groups of participants. For example, if you were studying the effects of organisation of material on learning, you could pre-test people's memory, and then pair each participant with a second participant with a very similar score. In this way, you would ensure that the two groups were very similar in respect of memory. This design is called a *matched groups design* and is similar to the repeated measures design. Both the matched groups and the repeated measures designs are examples of *related groups designs*. Although the idea of matched groups seems to overcome certain problems, the great practical difficulty comes in knowing that you have really matched individuals properly. The matched groups design also takes much longer and adds greatly to the inconvenience for the researcher and, more importantly, the inconvenience for the participants (who are frequently giving their time as volunteers).

The third and the most commonly used method of controlling for individual differences is to randomly assign participants to groups. Although this may seem crude, as long as your sample sizes are not very small, it is likely to be an effective method. It is very important that you really do randomly assign participants to conditions. You should be aware that many things that appear at first sight to be random turn out not to be so.

Before reading on, look at the following descriptions of methods of assigning participants to conditions, and decide which of these methods are truly random, and which are not.

1. First person to arrive is assigned to Group 1, second person is assigned to Group 2, third person to Group 1, etc.

2. First 10 people to arrive are assigned to Group 1, next 10 people to arrive are assigned to Group 2.

3. Participants asked to stand in a large group, then you draw a line approximately down the middle of the group dividing the participants into two groups.

4. All participants placed in alphabetical order of surname. Participants in the first half are placed in Group 1, participants in the second half are placed in Group 2.

---

[1] If you talk with your friends at university who study other subjects about the things that you have learned in your studies of psychology, they may be cynical and say 'Huh. How can you say that? Everyone is different.' To stop this happening, before you say anything, you should say 'Of course, everyone is different, but generally. . .'

5. Participants who need to leave early are in Group 1, other participants are in Group 2.

Which of those methods did you decide were truly random? The answer is none.

> **Crucial tip** Students use the word 'random' inappropriately more than almost any other word. Never use the word 'random' when you don't really mean random.

There are only two types of ways of assigning people to groups *randomly*. The first is to put the names of all participants in a hat, stir them very thoroughly and draw them out. The second is to toss a coin for each. (The hat and the coin do not have to be real, they can be computerised or constructed using random number tables, but the process must be the exact equivalent of using either a hat or a coin.)

Although randomisation would seem to be a rather crude method of dealing with participant variables, it is effective for ensuring that all groups are equivalent – especially when dealing with larger numbers. From the point of view of researchers and participants, it is very quick and easy to administer.

> **Crucial tip** When you carry out experiments of your own, you need to randomly assign participants to conditions, and you also need to describe how you carried out the random assignment in your report of the experiment.

Participant effects

In psychology, we have a special problem that is not encountered in other sciences. In chemistry, astronomy or biology the things that we are studying will usually sit still and allow us to investigate them. A frog, a star or a chemical reaction will carry on doing what they were doing, regardless of whether anyone is watching or not. This is not the case in psychology; as soon as people know that they are in a psychology experiment and are being investigated, they will start to behave differently. This makes psychology much more difficult than many other sciences.

When people find out that they are in a psychology experiment, thoughts occur such as:

'What is the psychologist really studying?'
'Am I behaving in a way that would be considered 'normal'?'
'Am I spoiling the experiment for them by behaving in this way?'

In addition, because of these thoughts, people will behave differently. This phenomenon was recognised by Orne, who wrote an influential and important paper in 1962 called 'On the social psychology of the social psychology experiment'. (Although Orne focused particularly on social psychology, the implications of his paper relate to many areas of psychology.) Orne said that we psychologists put people into different situations so that we can study them. What we sometimes forget is that being in a psychology experiment is a special kind of situation, and people may behave differently – people in psychology experiments do things that they would not normally do.

On one occasion, Orne asked some of his friends if they would mind doing five press-ups for him. The people he asked, naturally, said 'Why?' Then Orne asked people if they could spare five minutes for a psychology experiment. When people agreed Orne asked them if they would mind doing five press-ups for him. The people said 'Where?' The characteristics of the situation that make people behave in strange ways, or ways in which they would not normally behave, are called 'demand characteristics'.

What can you do to prevent participant effects? One method is to disguise the true nature of the experiment from the participant by providing them with as little information as possible. If they do not know what you are expecting or 'hoping for' they cannot change their behaviour to please you in such a way that it will ruin your experiment – there should be no 'good participant' effects. This commonly used procedure is called a 'single blind' procedure.

If you tell them nothing about the experiment, the participants will be unlikely to work out the hypothesis that you are investigating. However, this lack of knowledge will not stop them from guessing what your hypothesis *might* be and responding to that instead – and so their responses might well be even more random and bizarre. So, do not deny them all information. People are naturally suspicious, and people who have any knowledge of psychological research are especially suspicious. If you are conducting an experiment to examine the effects of attractiveness on judgements of intelligence, tell the participants that you are investigating judgements of intelligence. Tell the participants something about the area – just do not tell the participants the *precise* nature of your hypothesis. (We will come across this issue again when we consider ethical issues within psychological research in Chapter 6.)

Experimenter effects

In this section, we will look at experimenter effects as extraneous variables. Experimenter effects can introduce two kinds of extraneous variable – both systematic and random. In this section, we will first look at systematic extraneous variables introduced through experimenter effects, and then at random extraneous variables introduced through experimenter effects.

SYSTEMATIC EXPERIMENTER EFFECTS

A further difficulty that we have in psychology is that you and I (the researchers) are also people. And people find it difficult to be objective when there is a desired or expected outcome. When cars driven by two people collide, there is rarely agreement about why the collision occurred.

Similarly, researchers may not agree about what happened if they observe a particular behaviour. Imagine two psychologists watching two children at play. One of them, A, has a theory that suggests that the children behave aggressively toward one another. The second psychologist, B, has a theory that the children are friendly towards one another.

One child throws a ball towards another child. What the two psychologists write in their notes is shown in Figure 2.4.

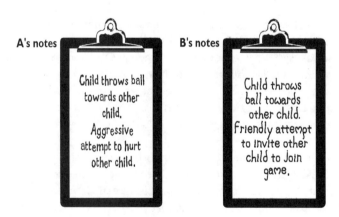

Figure 2.4: Two different psychologists' interpretation of the same incident.

Experimenters, as we have seen, are capable of interpreting the same behaviour differently. Subtle differences in experimenter behaviour can also alter the way in which participants behave. A set of instructions read out to participants could be read in different ways to different participants.

Compare:

> Please look at the following problems, thank you. **Work as QUICKLY as you can**. *Oh, but there is no time limit. Take as long as you need.*

> Please look at the following problems, thank you. *Work as quickly as you can*. There is **NO TIME LIMIT**. Take as **LONG** as you need.

In conclusion, how an experimenter behaves or perceives certain situations can have a systematic, or biasing, effect on our results.

On some occasions there may be deliberate and malicious attempts on the part of the experimenter to manipulate the experiment in the direction that supports their 'pet' hypothesis. However, it is much more likely that the researcher, while making every effort to be scrupulous and fair, will still give additional cues to participants without realising that this is what they are doing. If an experimenter wanted to make a deliberate and malicious attempt to manipulate an experiment, it is much easier to simply change the data.

Random experimenter effects

As we have seen, experimenters can introduce systemic extraneous variables (biases) into their experiments through their behaviour or their perception. Less serious, although much more common, is the introduction of random (non-systematic) extraneous variables. They could make a mistake in recording information or they could make an error in judgement. As we have seen above, an experimenter who is recording information may make errors. These may be judgement errors – they saw an act as aggressive when it was playful – or they may simply be clerical errors – they ticked the wrong box or wrote the wrong number down. In terms of behaviour, different experimenters may behave in slightly different ways – one may talk quickly, one may talk more slowly. They may have different regional accents, and this may alter perceptions of the experimenter. If a person has a Cockney accent, the participant may think them less trustworthy than a person with a Northern accent. (Call centres tend to be based in the North of England, because people find Northern English accents more trustworthy.) It is difficult, or even impossible, for a researcher to behave in an identical manner with every participant – and this may have some effect on the behaviour of the participants.

Section summary

Extraneous variables are variables that affect the dependent variable in our experiment and may mean that our experimental results mislead us. Extraneous variables come in two types: random extraneous variables and systematic extraneous variables (also known as biases). Random extraneous variables may have the effect of obscuring our results, but they will not mislead us because they affect all participants randomly. Systematic extraneous variables are much more problematic because they bias the results of our experiment.

We looked at four different types of extraneous variable: situation variables, participant variables, participant effects and experimenter effects. In any experiment, you should be aware of all of these effects and attempt to minimise them.

Section 5 — Designing the study

What are you studying?

This section looks at some of the issues in designing your study. There are a number of choices to be made, and any decision you make will have advantages and disadvantages which you need to be aware of. For certain experimental designs, you need to take many more precautions which we will consider here.

Why do you need to know how to design an experiment?

To test a hypothesis, we need to design and carry out a study. When you plan a study, you will need to make a large number of decisions. The decisions that need to be made do not necessarily have any specific right or wrong answers – there will be pros and cons to every answer. (Of course, some answers will be better than others, and some will be wrong, but none will be exactly correct.)

You are likely to be assessed on your understanding of experimental design, and your understanding of what the advantages and disadvantages of different designs might be.

1. You will be asked to design studies. In designing a study, you need to justify why you made the decisions that you did and why you rejected other options.

2. You might be given descriptions of studies and asked to evaluate the choices they made. You also might be asked to provide alternative designs and evaluate those choices.

Once a psychologist has proposed a hypothesis the next stage is to design an experiment or study which will test that hypothesis. We will look at two different issues in this section: the experimental setting (the field or the laboratory) and experimental design.

Field and laboratory studies

When designing a study a researcher has to decide whether to carry out the research as a laboratory study or as a field study. The choice of one technique over another often sacrifices the ability to collect clear data on some aspect of the problem. The choice of technique, therefore, will usually be a compromise.

> Crucial concept A *laboratory study* takes place in an environment where the researcher has a great deal of control over the surroundings – in a psychology laboratory.

> Crucial concept A *field study* takes place in an environment where the researcher does not have a great deal of control over the surroundings – outside a psychology laboratory, in the 'real world'.

In the laboratory environment an experimenter is able to eliminate or control possible *extraneous variables*, so the experimenter can be fairly confident that any changes that are measured in the dependent variable are caused by manipulations of the independent variable(s). For example, if we wanted to test participants' ability to solve two types of reasoning problem (one easy and one difficult) we might choose a laboratory study.

In some instances, however, a laboratory environment may be rather artificial. For example, a developmental psychologist might want to observe the way in which siblings play with a particular toy. Placing children in a laboratory situation would allow clear observations to be made without the children knowing that they were being observed. However, taking brothers and sisters out of their home environment and putting them into a laboratory situation might inhibit their natural play behaviour. In this instance, the experimenter couldn't be confident that the behaviour observed was not in some way attributable to the laboratory environment.

This observational study, therefore, might best be carried out in the *field*. This could involve the experimenter observing the children as they play at home. The home environment might promote more natural play behaviour than in the laboratory, but there is a risk of the children being inhibited by the presence of the experimenter. Here we can see how the choice of whether to carry out a laboratory study or field study may sometimes be a compromise.

Experimental designs

If you have decided that an experiment is the best approach to testing your hypothesis, then you need to design the experiment. Sometimes the choice of experimental design will be a very straightforward choice; on other occasions it will be more difficult to decide.

There are two major types of design that we will consider here: repeated measures and independent groups.

INDEPENDENT GROUPS DESIGN

> Crucial concept An *independent group* design (also known as a *between-participants* design) involves each participant being tested under only one level of the independent variable. This means that each condition of the experiment includes a different group of participants.

It is very important that participants are randomly assigned to the different conditions. If they are not randomly assigned, we cannot be sure that any differences which arise between the groups are not due to differences between the groups, and are due to the independent variable.

REPEATED MEASURES DESIGN

> Crucial concept A *repeated measures* design (also known as a *within-participants* design) involves each participant being tested under *all* levels of the independent variable. This means that each condition of the experiment includes the same group of participants.

With the repeated measures design each participant is tested under *all* levels of the independent variable(s). This means that each person is tested on more than one occasion. Repeated measures designs are sometimes known as within-subjects designs, because we are making a comparison within one group of people.

The major advantage of the repeated measures design is that each subject effectively acts as their own control – this means that fewer participants are required to achieve the same degree of statistical power (see Chapter 7 for a discussion of statistical power).

PROBLEMS WITH REPEATED MEASURES DESIGNS

Some problems can arise when using a repeated measures design. Keren (1993) identified them as follows:

- *Practice effects.* A practice effect occurs when a participant has practised a task and will be better at it the second time they do it. If we ask people to solve some anagrams as quickly as they can, the second time they do it they will be more practised at solving anagrams and will do it more quickly.

- *Sensitisation.* If you are assessing factors that might change people's attitudes or beliefs, you might ask people the same questions on two occasions. However, participants may keep their answers similar – they might want to seem consistent. If I said that people who are caught in possession of cannabis should be automatically fined £100, whatever you say to me I will remember that I said that and will not change my statement, even if you do succeed in changing my beliefs.

- *Carryover effects.* A carryover effect occurs when the fact that an individual has already done part of the experiment will affect how they perform in the next part. The most important carryover effect is fatigue. By the second or third time a person is running through an experimental procedure, they are likely to be getting bored or tired. Some treatments (for example drugs) may remain in the system of the participant, or have a long-term effect. Carryover effects will also occur if the experimental procedure involves a deception that is revealed to the participant as part of the procedure. Some studies on memory ask a participant to read a list of words and answer questions on those words. When they have done this, the participant is asked to recall as many of the words as possible. A repeated measures design would be no use at all here because the second time the participant was asked to undertake the task, they would expect their memory to be tested and would therefore make a much greater attempt to recall the words.

SOLUTIONS TO THE PROBLEMS

Counterbalancing and randomisation

Counterbalancing and randomisation are two precautions that can be taken against the problems identified above.

> Crucial concept *Counterbalancing* involves equal numbers of participants doing the conditions in each of the possible orders of the conditions.

This is very straightforward when we have just two conditions. Half of the participants do one condition first, and the other half do the other condition first. You would divide your participants (randomly, of course) into two groups, A and B. Group A would do condition 1 first, and Group B would do condition 2 first.

With more than two conditions, things become a little more complicated. We will look at an example with three conditions.

You split the sample (again randomly) into three groups, Group A, Group B and Group C. Group A carry out the conditions in the order 1, 2, 3, Group B carry out the tasks in the order 2, 3, 1, and Group C carry out the conditions in the order 3, 1, 2.

Before reading on can you think of any problems arising from this method of counterbalancing?

The problem is that condition 2 always follows condition 1, and condition 3 always follows condition 2. It might be the case that there is some 'carry-over' from one condition to the next, and because the conditions always follow the same order, may be a systematic bias – affecting one condition more than it affects the other conditions. It is possible to avoid these problems with an alternative method, *randomisation*.

> Crucial concept   When using *randomisation*, the conditions for each participant are placed into a random order.

Randomisation ensures that any systematic effects of order should be minimised, if not eliminated. In a study of memory, you might be interested in presenting participants with two types of words to see which type is more likely to be remembered. If you were counterbalancing, you would present first one list and then the other (varying the order). For this type of study, a better approach may be randomisation, where you mix the words together and present them in a random order, which would differ for each participant. Writing each word on a card and then shuffling the cards is the easiest way to do this, although it can also be done using a computer-based presentation.

> Crucial tip   If you have carried out a study using a repeated measures design, it is vital that you use counterbalancing. When you are writing a practical report, if you used a repeated measures design, you need to describe how you counterbalanced.

Pre-practice

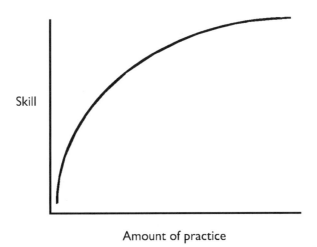

Figure 2.5: A typical learning curve

The second precaution which can be taken when using a repeated measures design is to pre-practise. Most people go through a learning curve where skill develops rapidly at first and then more slowly, as shown in Figure 2.5. If each participant practises the task before the experiment, the effects of practice (and of different practice between conditions) will be minimised.

Section summary

In this section, we have considered some of the issues that arise when designing experiments. First, we considered the issue of experimental setting: experiments can be set in the laboratory for greater control, or in the field for greater realism. The next issue that we considered was the issue of using an independent groups design or a repeated measures design. A repeated measures design requires fewer participants than an independent groups design, but raises problems with practice effects, sensitisation and carryover effects. Sometimes precautions such as counterbalancing, randomisation and pre-practice can eliminate these problems.

Further reading

Many texts which discuss experimental design also discuss the associated statistics (there is nothing wrong with that – the two cannot really be separated, but you the reader are only on Chapter 2 here). If you don't mind this, then a nice little book on design is *Relating Statistics and Experimental Design: An Introduction* by Levin (published by Sage).

Most introductory books on research methods and statistics look at experimental design. Your lecturers may already have recommended a book to you, but if they have not, you could have a look at *Research Methods in Psychology* by Heiman (published by Houghton Mifflin).

A very clearly written book is *Methods of Research in Social Psychology* by Aronson et al. (published by McGraw Hill). Don't let the social psychology in the title put you off (if it were about to) – what they say applies to most experimental research in psychology.

If you are interested in going into much more detail on research in field settings you could look at *Quasi-experimentation* by Cook and Campbell (published by Houghton Mifflin).

NON-EXPERIMENTAL
DESIGNS

Chapter summary
Studying this Chapter will help you to:

- Understand the importance of the experimental method, particularly in relation to causality.
- Be able to describe and evaluate a range of non-experimental methods in psychology.

How will you be assessed on this?

You are likely to be tested on your knowledge of experiments in two different ways:

1. As part of your practical work you will need to know how to design and carry out non-experimental research.

2. As well as doing your own research, you might be asked to read about research that has been carried out, and then make a critical evaluation of that research. If you want to evaluate a piece of experimental research, you can discuss the possibility of testing the hypothesis using non-experimental research. If you read about a piece of non-experimental research, you can discuss the possibility of testing the hypothesis using experimental research.

Crucial concepts

These are the key terms you will meet in this Chapter:

Case studies	Correlation and (spurious) causation
Correlation	Experiments and cause and effect
Quasi-experiment	Non-equivalent control group design
Surveys	Interruption time-series design

Section I — Experimental versus non-experimental research

What are you studying?

This section starts off by reconsidering experiments – which seems curious for a chapter on non-experimental designs (especially when the last chapter was all about experiments), but we do this to contrast the non-experimental research methods with experiments.

In the last chapter, we spent a long time describing experimental design – but we didn't look at why experiments are so common, or why experiments are used more than many other types of research design.

Studies in psychology can be divided into two types – experimental studies and non-experimental studies. The distinction is important: take care not to use the word 'experiment' when you mean 'research study'.

We will begin this chapter by having a reminder of what we mean by experimental design, and then we will have a look at the advantages of the experimental method. However, all is not rosy in the world of experiments, and we will have a look at some of the problems associated with experiments, and some of the alternative designs.

Experiments

Crucial concept   An *experiment* in psychology is carried out to investigate the causal effect of one or more variables (the independent variables) on another variable (the dependent variable).

To do an experiment the researcher changes an independent variable, and then measures the effect of this change on the dependent variable. Seeking out naturally occurring variations in the independent variables is one way to do a study, but studying naturally occurring variations is *not* an experiment.

Often an independent variable will have two values or levels, although sometimes an experiment may involve an independent variable with more than two levels. Sometimes one of the levels will be described as being a *control* group. This control group will act as a baseline to which the other groups can be compared. A control group may be used with one or more experimental groups, but not every experiment has a control group. Experiments may also have more than one independent variable.

CAUSE AND EFFECT: THE ADVANTAGE OF EXPERIMENTS

The great advantage of experiments over other study designs is that, with an experimental design, you can demonstrate cause and effect relationships. A psychological experiment involves two or more equivalent groups of people. First, each group undergoes some sort of procedure, and then a measurement is then taken of the effect of that procedure on the groups. After the experiment, any differences between the groups must be caused either by the procedure that we carried out or by chance. If we did the experiment properly, there is *no other* explanation. If we eliminate or at least minimise chance, we are left with the explanation that the differences between the groups were caused by the differences between the procedures that we carried out on each respective group.

You find this *precise* relationship between cause and effect only by carrying out an experiment. (Actually, this isn't the whole truth — if you want to know more, see below.)

The truth about cause and effect...

Unfortunately for you, the student, the whole issue of causality is surprisingly complex. Philosophers have argued for a long time about precisely what is meant by the term 'cause', and authors of some statistics (and philosophy) books have tried to avoid the problem by never using the word 'cause' in their texts.

To make life even more difficult, different researchers and different tutors do not agree about this issue. You need to be aware that some people take a very strict line, and say that without an experiment statements about cause and effect can never be justly made. Others take a less strict line and say that statements about cause and effect relationships can be made occasionally, if care is taken (yes, you do not get any less strict than that). I hold that causal statements can be made if care is taken and appropriate techniques are used, but your tutors may not agree. Your tutors are the ones who assess your work, so while you are a student, you should take care to follow whatever they say.

We don't have the space here to go into when you can and cannot make causal statements. If you would like to know more about the arguments, see Cook and Campbell (1979), Miles and Shevlin (2001), Chapter 5, or Pearl (2000). (Cook and Campbell is the definitive book on these issues, Miles and Shevlin give an overview of some of the issues from the perspective of correlational designs, and Pearl is a somewhat dense and mathematical, but informative, treatment of the issues.)

Alternatives to experiments

You should not underestimate the usefulness of the experimental method in determining cause and effect relationships. However, an experiment is not always the most appropriate approach, as we shall see. Sometimes it is not possible to carry out a true experiment because, for practical or for ethical reasons, it is impossible to manipulate the independent variable. Sometimes an experiment is not a useful way to answer the question that we are asking.

We will have a look at some examples of studies that could not be carried out using experiments. Recently researchers (e.g. Wareing, Fisk and Murphy, 2000) have been studying the psychological effects of long-term ecstasy use. While it would be nice to do an experiment to investigate this problem, it is not possible. We would have to take a large group of people and ask some of them to take ecstasy on a regular basis and the other half to abstain. However, if we do not do this, it is very hard to say that any difference between people who have taken ecstasy and people who have not taken ecstasy is caused by the ecstasy. There may have been other differences between the users and the non-users which determined whether they would become ecstasy users. However, just because we cannot do an experiment does not mean that we cannot try to answer the questions we might have about the psychological consequences of ecstasy.

A second example of a situation where we would be unable to carry out an experiment would occur if we were interested in examining the effects of personality and individual differences – what kind of people are more (or less) likely to do certain things. Many studies have been carried out which have examined the reasons for the use, and non-use, of condoms by young people. Suppose we are interested in examining the relationship between personality and condom use. An experiment would be impossible: we cannot alter some people's personalities and then see how the alteration affects their use of condoms. Instead, we must study many individuals to discover their condom use habits and their personalities, and then analyse our findings to see if there is any relationship between these two (as done by Wulfert et al., 1999).

There are occasions an experiment would not answer the question of interest. If research is at an early stage, it might be difficult to precisely formulate the hypotheses of interest. When Piaget was interested in studying the moral development of children, he used a non-experimental approach to explore the kinds of hypotheses that he might want to test later. He started by playing games with children. While he was playing games, he would start to deliberately break the rules to see how the children reacted. From their reactions, he was able to formulate precise hypotheses which he could then test experimentally.

Sometimes an event or an individual may be of a rare type or even unique. In this case, the individual might be the subject of a test of a hypothesis, but the test cannot take the form of an experiment. Polledri (1997) describes a case study of a course of therapy with a 'potential serial killer' (who was being held in a regional secure unit having murdered his mother while an adolescent). Attempts were made to change the patient's behaviour by changing his beliefs and attitudes. Working with this individual in considerable depth provided greater understanding of that individual and, hopefully, of potential murderers in general.

Section summary

In this section, we have considered experimental designs and looked particularly at their main advantage – the ability to make causal inferences from experimental research. We have also looked at some occasions when experiments are not appropriate, either because it is not possible to carry out an experiment, or because an experiment would not allow us to answer the questions that we are interested in.

Section 2   Non-experimental designs

What are you studying?

In this section we will describe and evaluate four non-experimental designs: quasi-experimental designs, correlational designs, case studies and surveys.

Quasi-experimental designs

> Crucial concept   In a *quasi-experiment*, a researcher finds naturally occurring groups – they do not assign people to the different groups.

The main difference between the quasi-experimental design and the true experimental design is that with the former, participants are *not* randomly assigned to experimental groups. Instead, the experimenter may assign participants to groups according to age, sex, weight, nationality or some behavioural characteristic (for example, smokers and non-smokers). Alternatively, a researcher might observe the effects of events such as an accident or a change in someone's life circumstances.

Quasi-experimental designs come in two types.

NON-EQUIVALENT CONTROL GROUP DESIGNS

The non-equivalent control group design is the equivalent of the independent groups experimental design that was discussed in Chapter 2. When an independent groups experimental design is used, the participants are randomly assigned to conditions or levels of the independent variable. Sometimes it is not possible to assign participants randomly to different conditions. This might occur for several reasons.

- The independent variable of interest may be some characteristic of the person, such as age or sex, which we cannot alter.
- It might be unethical to assign participants to conditions, for example we might be interested in the effects of women drinking while pregnant.
- The independent variable of interest might be a behavioural characteristic of a person, such as a smoking habit, which we cannot alter.

Because we didn't assign participants to conditions, we cannot be sure that the independent variable was the cause of any differences that we find – there is always the possibility that an extraneous variable had a systematic effect and was the actual cause of the difference. We can't, in other words, be sure that the control group is equivalent to the experimental group. To reduce the problems of non-equivalence as much as possible, it is usual to compare the different groups in other ways, and ensure that they are as similar as possible.

INTERRUPTED TIME-SERIES DESIGNS

The interrupted time-series design is the equivalent of the repeated measures design (discussed in Chapter 2), but as with the non-equivalent control group design, the researchers do not control when the intervention occurs.

When an interrupted time-series design is used, participants are observed or their behaviour is measured on a number of occasions prior to some event. After the event, the participants are observed or measured again, usually more than once. The aim of the research is to investigate the effect of the event. This design would be used to study the impact of an event such as redundancy or pregnancy.

Correlation

> Crucial concept   A *correlation* is used to measure the relationship between two variables.

Correlational studies are the most common type of non-experimental design. A correlational design is used to determine whether or not there is a relationship between two variables which we cannot manipulate (as in an experimental design). Correlational designs are commonly employed in the applied branches of psychology (clinical, health, educational, occupational) where the variables of interest will be real-world phenomena that we cannot manipulate.

WHY USE CORRELATION?

The advantage of the correlational design is its flexibility. We can collect data on any type of variable, then look for relationships. Correlations are commonly used where characteristics of people are the variables of interest and the values of these variables are continuous rather than categorical. In psychology, the types of variable that are studied using correlations are individual characteristics such as intelligence, attitudes and personality dimensions.

Riemann et al. (1993) carried out a correlational study. They were interested in how a personality dimension known as 'openness to experience' related to adherence to right-wing political ideology. They collected data on *openness* and on *right-wing orientation* and found a negative relationship between the two variables. This finding suggests that people who have lower scores on the openness questionnaire are more likely to endorse right-wing ideas. It does not suggest that there is a causal relationship between these two variables, or that being open to experience is a cause of being left wing.

Correlational research design enables us to look at historical data that other people have already collected and use those data for our analysis – we do not need to go out and collect the data ourselves. Herrnstein and Murray (1994) used a very large American study called the National Longitudinal Survey of Youth (NLSY) to analyse data about a very wide range of variables, including intelligence, poverty, crime, race and pregnancy. They did not need to go and collect these data themselves, they were already collected and made available to academics. (It should be noted that Herrnstein and Murray's analysis has been questioned, particularly in relation to the causal conclusions that they drew.)

Correlational analysis can be extended in a number of ways into more complex analyses that consider relationships between many variables at once.

PROBLEMS WITH CORRELATION

The main disadvantage of the correlational technique is that you cannot say for sure that you know that one variable, A, is causing the other variable, B. Sometimes it may seem obvious that A is causing B, but when you think harder, you realise that this is not necessarily the case. Maybe B is causing A, or it may be that C (which we do not necessarily know about) is causing both A and B. It is very easy to come to a wrong conclusion which the evidence does not justify.

Consider the following examples:

- Children who are brought up by loving, tender parents have higher self-esteem.

- People who watch more violent television programmes are more likely to commit violent crime.
- Unemployed people are more likely to suffer from mental illness.

If you are like most people, you will leap to the following conclusions:

- Parental behaviour causes higher self-esteem.
- Violent television causes violent behaviour.
- Unemployment causes mental illness.

But the evidence in the first set of statements does not justify the conclusions in the second set of statements. While these statements are not necessarily untrue, we do not have the evidence to be able to say that they are true. And, as scientists, we do not want to say things unless we know them to be true (or at least are pretty sure). Whenever you read that there is a relationship between two variables (let us call them A and B), with the implication that one of them causes the other (i.e. that A causes B), you should always think of the alternatives.

> **Someone is claiming:**
> **A causes B**
>
> **Is it possible that the direction is reversed:**
> **B causes A**
>
> **or even that something else (we will call it C) is causing both of them?**
> **C causes A and B**

Before you read ahead, think about the three examples above, and try to decide whether it is possible that the direction of causality is reversed, or that some third factor (C) is causing both effects.

First, we said that children who are brought up by loving, tender parents tend to have higher self-esteem. We assumed that parental behaviour caused self-esteem to change. First, let us consider the alternative, that child's self-esteem causes parental behaviour. Could a child's self-esteem alter parental behaviour? This is possible – parents behave differently towards different sorts of children. A parent is likely to behave differently towards a calm, happy, well-mannered child than they would behave towards a child who misbehaved. Could differences between Bart and Lisa Simpson be because of differential treatment from parents? If you were those parents, which child would you be more inclined to try to involve in extra activities. Would you buy a saxophone for Lisa, or Bart?

Now we will consider the third option, that something else – the third factor, C – is causing parental behaviour and the child's behaviour. Here there are many choices that we could make, one of them being genes. A parent who has a genetic inclination to behave in a particular way will behave in that way with their child and may also pass those genes onto the child. Thus there may be a relationship between the parent's behaviour and the child's behaviour, which has nothing to do with the interaction between them.

Our next example was that people who behave violently are likely to watch violent television. We easily jump to the conclusion that watching violent television causes violent behaviour, but (as always) there are other explanations for the relationship. First, could it be that engaging in violent behaviour causes people to want to watch violent programmes on the television? If you are with a peer group who engage in violent behaviour, you might find that this is enjoyable and exciting. If you do this, you may then like to watch such violence on the television, to be reminded of the enjoyment that you had.

Of course, it might be a third variable which is causing both of these behaviours. It might be possible that you feel that you have not received the opportunities that other people have had and that you are frustrated by the life that you are forced to lead. Because of this frustration, you might engage in violent behaviour. You might also like to watch escapist violence on the television, to help you to forget about your lot.

Finally, we said that unemployment causes mental illness. This sounds very feasible, because being unemployed combines long-term stress and worry, along with long periods of boredom and inactivity. However, is there an alternative explanation? First the direction of causality may be reversed. It is possible that mental illness may lead to unemployment – a person whose thinking is disorganised and chaotic, a symptom of schizophrenia, may have trouble in an interview situation. A person who is suffering from depression may have difficulty motivating themselves to get to work on time, and may therefore be late for an interview and unable to convince a potential employer of their enthusiasm and dynamism, and so be unlikely to get a job.

There could be a third factor. If a person has many difficulties in life, ill-health in their family, unpleasant housing and few friends, then that person may be prone to mental illness and may also find it impossible to maintain their responsibilities at home and at work, and hence lose their job.

Case studies

> Crucial concept   A *case study* is an in-depth study of either one individual or a small number of individuals, or of an organisation.

ADVANTAGES

A case study is useful when the subject of the study is rare or unique, and it is also useful when we want to study something in great depth.

A problem with research methods other than case studies is that they tend to lump people together into one block, ignoring the fact that every individual is unique and has a different story to tell. If we take a group of people who are depressed, each one will have a very different history and background. Different things will have affected them in different ways, and each one will be unique. If we put them into one group which we then investigate using a standard research technique, we will lose some information. By studying one person in depth we might be able to find out much more about the origins of depression than we could by studying a larger group of people.

Sometimes a case study is used because a case is rare or unique. One such example is that of serial killers. There are very few true serial killers, therefore when a serial killer is caught who is willing to talk to a psychologist or psychiatrist about their motivation and reasons for what they have done, it may provide valuable information for the future.

DISADVANTAGES

The main disadvantage of the case study is that because it is only carried out on one individual, or a small number of individuals, we have no idea how far we can generalise the results. The case that we choose to study in depth may be very similar to all other cases, or it may be completely different. In the case of a serial killer, conclusions that apply to just one person may lead detectives off the correct trail and up a blind alley.

Griffiths (1997) wrote a case study report of a woman who was, he claimed, addicted to exercise. He said that there had been a great deal of speculation that exercise addiction might exist, but little firm evidence. Griffiths presented a detailed description of the woman, and the evidence that she satisfied all of the criteria to be diagnosed as suffering from exercise addiction. This case study, then, presents evidence to demonstrate the exercise addiction is a reality.

Barlow and Harrison (1996) carried out a case study of an organisation that provided support and counselling to young people who suffered from arthritis. Here the aim of the study was not to test any theory, but rather to explore what people thought about different aspects of the support and counselling which was provided. The lessons learned from this study could be used to help people develop support networks for arthritis or other conditions.

Surveys

> **Crucial concept** A *survey* aims to find out the current level of the value of something in a population.

Surveys are comparatively rare in psychology. Although many studies may look like surveys, they are actually correlational designs or quasi-experiments. A survey aims to take a snapshot of a population at any one time and report on the findings. Theories and hypotheses in psychological research rarely make statements about the current state of any situation – they usually make statements about differences or relationships between variables. A survey, on the other hand, looks at the current state of different aspects of a population.

Surveys are sometimes used in psychology to assess the current state of a situation to determine whether there is a problem that needs to be addressed. Fisher (1999) carried out a survey of 10,000 12–15 year olds to assess the current level of gambling behaviour amongst them. She found that 13% had spent money on the National Lottery in the previous week, and 19% had spent their own money on fruit machines in the previous week.

Surveys are not necessarily of people – surveys of many different things can be carried out. Taylor and Stern (1997) surveyed television advertisements to examine the proportion of people in those adverts who were Asian-Americans and the roles these Asian-Americans played. They found that Asian-Americans were featured fairly frequently, but often in background or work roles. They very rarely appeared in leisure roles or at home.

Psychological literature is sometimes the subject of surveys. Literature surveys come in two types – the first and most common is a review of the literature, the literature being a large number of studies which have all examined the same hypothesis. Bond and Smith (1996) carried out a literature survey to look at 133 different studies that had examined conformity to large groups. They found that the results of such studies varied over time and between countries. The second type is a survey of the literature to see what sorts of techniques people are using in published studies. Tennen, Hall and Affleck (1995) were interested in seeing how different researchers had been measuring depression. They looked at articles that had been published in the *Journal of Personality and Social Psychology*. From their survey, their conclusion was that the researchers whose work they had surveyed had not used adequate methods of measuring depression. Of course, some of those researchers disagreed with their conclusions – see Kendall and Flannery-Schroeder (1995) and Weary, Edwards and Jacobson, (1995).

Section summary

This section has considered and evaluated four non-experimental designs. A quasi-experimental design is used where we have naturally occurring groups or events which we cannot manipulate. A correlational design is used to compare the relationship between two measures. We considered the problem of causality in relation to correlations in some detail — looking at examples of occasions when it is tempting to make inappropriate causal statements based on correlational data. Case studies are an in-depth investigation of one individual, used either when there are only a small number of cases available or when you want to try to gain a more detailed, holistic picture of an individual. Surveys are rare in psychology and are used to take a 'snapshot' of a population at one time.

Further reading

If you are involved in conducting surveys, Sage publish 'The Survey Kit', a collection of nine books edited by Fink, looking at all aspects of surveys, from design, sampling and data collection to reporting.

For other aspects of non-experimental research, one of the best books is *Real World Research* by Robson (published by Blackwell).

CHAPTER 4

MEASUREMENT
IN PSYCHOLOGY

Chapter summary

Studying this Chapter will help you to:

- Understand the problems of measurement in psychology.
- Understand ways of describing measures in terms of their level of measurement.
- Understand the importance of reliability and validity in psychological measurement.
- Be familiar with, and be able to evaluate, different methods of data collection.

Why do you need to know this?

Why do we have a chapter on measurement?

We have a whole chapter on 'measurement in psychology'. Why a whole chapter on measurement? Because measurement in psychology has special difficulties and is a special subject in itself. The branch of psychology associated with measurement is known as 'psychometrics' and it is a large and important area of psychological research. There are several academic journals devoted to the subject (*Psychometrika, Applied Psychological Measurement, Educational and Psychological Measurement*), and many advanced courses in psychology contain a module on psychometric theory.

When you design your research projects, you need to think long and hard about how to measure the construct (thing) that you are interested in. It is very easy to think that you are measuring something well, and then find that what you really measured was completely different.

Crucial concepts

These are the key terms you will meet in this Chapter:

Ethics	Physiological measures
Internal consistency	Psychometrics
Interview	Questionnaire
Levels of measurement	Reliability
Nominal, ordinal, interval and ratio scales	Self-report
Observation	Survey
Observation reactivity	Validity

Section I   Introduction

What are you studying?

In this section we introduce some ideas about measurement in psychology. In particular, we consider why we need to think so hard about measurement in psychology.

> Crucial concept *Psychometrics* is the branch of psychology concerned with studying and using measurement techniques.

In this chapter we are going to look at some aspects of psychometrics. The word psychometrics has two sources – *psycho*, meaning mind, and *metric*, meaning measurement. As we shall see, this need for a branch of psychology that deals with measurement arises for two reasons. The first reason is the difficulty in identifying what we really want to measure. The second is that after we have identified what we want to measure, we have the problem of how to measure properly this thing or construct that we have identified. Whatever method of research you use, you will be collecting data as a means of measuring some effect. All of the methods of research that we examined in the previous two chapters involve the collection of data, and this chapter is all about the different ways that you can do it.

Difficulty in defining the construct

The first problem in measurement is to define the construct that we want to measure.

In most sciences, if we want to measure something, it has a physical reality and we are sure that it exists. In psychology, we are interested in mental events or mental processes, but we cannot see these things or even be sure that they exist.

Consider two examples of words that are used to describe characteristics that people might have:

- aggression;
- intelligence.

We may decide to carry out a study to investigate these characteristics. However, do they really exist? Let's consider an example.

Aggression. Some people are more aggressive than others. Most people would agree with that statement, but what does that statement mean? Some people who are aggressive will act violently towards people. It is pretty clear that these people are more aggressive than others. But does aggression necessarily imply physical violence? Some people can be quietly aggressive – they might sulk aggressively – they deliberately stop talking and act hurt in an attempt to try to upset people. They are passively aggressive. Other people may act aggressively in places where they may be judged favourably for it – some students will aggressively try to answer questions in seminars or aggressively try to finish their statistics exercises before others, but never dream of hitting anybody. We may use the word *aggression* to describe any or all of these behaviours, so is it clear that we are always talking about the same thing when we use the word *aggression*?

So, the first problem that we have is to determine that a psychological construct exists. The next problem is how do we go about actually measuring this thing which we believe exists? We will turn to this problem now.

Difficulties in measuring the construct

How do we find out how intelligent someone is? Intelligence cannot be measured with a measuring jug, a ruler or a scale. So, to find out how intelligent you are, I give you an intelligence test. But which intelligence test? There are many available, each of them measuring slightly different abilities. Some may be more dependent on verbal skills; some may depend more on non-verbal skills. Some are more appropriate for children; some are more appropriate for adults. Some have a time limit, some do not. Therefore there is more than one concept of *intelligence*.

A student of chemistry can talk about a quantity of water, a student of biology can talk about the weight of a frog, and a student of physics can talk about the brightness of a star. When they do this, everyone else who studies the subject will know exactly what they are talking about. This is not the case in psychology. When you write practical reports and talk about concepts like intelligence or aggression, you must explain exactly what you are talking about, and how you went about measuring that concept. You might also have to justify your choice of the method you used – not because the way you did it was wrong, but you need to tell the reader why you chose that method, from among all of the possible methods.

First, you must define the way in which you measured whatever it was you measured. Here, psychologists turn to 'operational definitions'. An operational definition is a definition that describes the construct through the processes that were used to measure it – what you actually did in the process of measurement. Because we cannot be sure that we were really measuring what we wanted to be measuring, we need to be very precise about how it was done. Only if you state very precisely *what you did* can a reader clearly evaluate your work.

Crucial tip   An operational definition states the *operations* that were used to make a measurement. It tells the reader about the process – this is vital to understanding what was really measured.

As we saw previously, it is difficult to define what is meant by aggression. If you say in your research report that you measured 'aggression', you are not being specific enough about what you did. Even saying specifically that you measured 'physical aggression' is still not sufficient. Your report needs to say something like:

> Physical aggression was defined as the number of times, within the 15-minute observation period, that each child committed a physically aggressive act. A physically aggressive act was defined as an attempt by one child to cause pain to another child by physical means. This includes all incidences of hitting, slapping, kicking or pinching, biting or scratching. Actions that caused pain, but which were not judged to have this as their primary intention, were not considered to be aggressive acts.

You then may want to describe, in some detail, acts which were considered aggressive and acts which were not considered to be aggressive, and explain why you decided to put the various acts into the *aggressive* or *not aggressive* category.

This may seem long-winded, but it is *vital* that you give a detailed definition such as the one above. If you do not give definitions this accurate, the reader will not be able to understand what you actually did.

Section summary

In this section were have introduced some ideas about measurement. We saw that there were two special problems that we have when we want to measure something in psychology. The first problem is that we cannot define the construct that we are talking about – we are talking about mental events and processes, and we need to make sure that we are all talking about the same thing. The second problem we have is that psychological constructs cannot be measured directly – it is difficult to measure a psychological construct, even when we have defined it.

Section 2   Levels of measurement

What are you studying?

In this section we will examine the four different levels of measurement that are used in psychological research. Understanding these levels of measurement is crucial to understanding the measurement process.

Crucial concept   The *level of measurement* of a variable informs us about the meaning of the relationships between numbers on a scale.

Since experiments in psychology are concerned with the collection of data, and data are the result of measurements, it is important to have an understanding of the types of scales that we use for the type of data we collect. The choice of measuring scale will determine the type of statistical tests that we can perform on the data. A very important series of articles by Stevens (1946, 1951) introduced the idea that there are four categories of scales or levels of measurement that are used in psychology experiments. These are: *nominal scales*, *ordinal scales*, *interval scales* and *ratio scales*. If we don't know the level of measurement, we don't know what the numbers are telling us. (This sounds like a rather difficult, abstract idea, but it should make sense if you read on.)

Crucial tip   A good way of remembering these is to take the initial letters from each word to form the word NOIR (French for black).

Nominal scales

Crucial concept   *Nominal data* are data that record *categories*.

The *nominal* level of measurement is often also known as *categorical* data. With this type of data observations are sorted into discrete, mutually exclusive categories. For example, keeping a record of the sex of each participant in an experiment is recording data at the nominal level. Males could be put into Category 1 and females into Category 2. Equally, you could do the reverse and put females into Category 1. The numbers 1 and 2 have no consequence except as labels. This *nominal scale* ranges from 1 to 2. As you can see, the actual numbers under which people or observations are classified are quite arbitrary. That is, the nominal number 2 in this example isn't greater or better than 1, it is merely *different*. As this is the case, calculating the mean or arithmetical average (the sum of the scores divided by the number of scores) would, since the scores are only names or labels, be meaningless. Categorising people according to favourite food, eye colour and postal district are other examples of the use of nominal scales.

Ordinal scales

Crucial concept   *Ordinal data* record information about the rank order of scores.

If objects or individuals are put into a rank order, we are using an *ordinal* scale. Data sorted in this way are sometimes also referred to as ordered categorical data. For example, an experimenter might ask you to rank your five favourite TV programmes into an order of preference – so that 1 signifies your most favourite and 5 signifies you least favourite. The data collected would be measurement at the ordinal level. The *ordinal scale* in this example ranges from 1 to 5.

You cannot assume that the differences in preference between TV programmes are always equal. That is, you might like your second favourite almost as much as you like your favourite, whereas you might prefer your third a long way ahead of your fourth favourite. Another example of ordinal data could be a list of the first, second and third order runners in a race to cross the finish line. The runner who crosses the line first could be a long way ahead of the runner who crosses the line second, while the second position could be only just ahead of the third. In other words, ordinal scales *do not have equal intervals*. As with nominal scales, therefore, you *usually* should not add values from an ordinal scale or perform other mathematical operations on those data.

Interval scales

> Crucial concept *Interval scales* tell us about the order of data points and the size of the intervals in between data points.

Interval data represents a much higher level of measurement than ordinal data. When data are measured on an interval scale, we know about the rank order (as with ordinal data), but we also know about the intervals – that is the differences. When we measured data on an ordinal scale we did not know anything about the distance between a score of 1 and a score of 2 – we did not know the size of the interval. When we measure numbers on an interval scale, we know that the distance – the interval – between the scores 1 and 2 is the same as the distance between 2 and 3.

The centigrade scale of temperature measurement is an example of an *interval* scale. The intervals between adjacent values in the centigrade scale are equal: it is reasonable to add and subtract the numbers on the centigrade scale. For example a temperature change of 10°C from 10°C to 20°C is exactly the same size as a temperature change of 10°C from 30°C to 40°C. We can also say that the difference in temperature between 40°C and 20°C is twice as much as the *difference* in temperature between 60°C and 50°C. However, interval scales do not have an absolute zero point. For example, 0 centigrade does *not* mean that the thermometer is measuring no heat at all: the 0 mark is simply a point on the scale.

Ratio scales

> Crucial concept A *ratio scale* is an interval scale with a true zero point.

The ratio scale has all the properties of the interval scale – equal intervals that can be added and subtracted. The important difference is that the ratio scale, unlike the interval scale, *does* have a true zero point. The implication of having a true zero point is that numbers on the scale, as well as being added and subtracted, can be multiplied and divided – you can say that one measurement was twice as big as another. You can't do this with a scale which doesn't have a true zero – 20°C is not twice as hot as 10°C (if you aren't convinced that this is true, tell me what is twice as hot [or cold] as 0°C). As an example of a ratio scale, consider the measurement of response times in a psychology experiment. The ratio scale has an absolute zero (e.g. a clock starts ticking at 0 seconds) and we can determine the ratios of values. For example, a participant in an experiment who took 10 seconds to respond to a stimulus can be said to have taken twice as long as a participant who took 5 seconds to respond (a ratio of 2 to 1). The distinction in psychology between interval and ratio measures is usually unimportant – ratio scales are treated as if they were interval.

Table 4.1 contains a summary of the levels of measurement (adapted from Stevens, 1951).

Scale	What do we know	What does it tell us	Examples
Nominal	Equal versus not equal	The same, or not the same	Shoe colour
Ordinal	Order	Above or below	Order in a race
Interval	Equality of intervals	The amount above or a certain amount below	Temperature (Celsius)
Ratio	Equality of ratios	The amount, and the proportion, above and below	Time (seconds)

Table 4.1: Levels of measurement.

Interval and ratio data are sometimes grouped together and referred to as *cardinal data* or *continuous data*.

It is possible to convert data from one level of measurement to another, but only in one direction. If you have data measured on a ratio scale you can convert them to interval data, by ignoring the zero. If you have data that are measured on a ratio scale you can convert them to ordinal data by converting them to ranks. If you have data that are measured on an ordinal scale, you can convert them to nominal data by grouping them into 'high' or 'low' categories. However, this is normally a bad thing to do – you can convert in one direction, but you cannot convert in the other direction, because the conversions that I have described involve discarding information, which cannot be retrieved.

Section summary
This section has examined the four levels of measurement: nominal, ordinal, interval, and ratio, and given examples of their use.

Section 3	Reliability and validity

What are you studying?
It is important that measures in psychology are both reliable and valid. We will look at two different ways of assessing reliability. Validity is the second important property of a measure – we will look at three different ways of assessing validity.

Reliability

Crucial concept   *Reliability* is the ability of a measure to give consistent scores.

When we say that a person or a car is reliable, we mean that we can predict to some extent what they are going to do. We know the person will turn up on time, and we know the car will start. Much the same is said of a measure in psychology. If a measure is reliable, we know that it is a good measure and that it will do what we expect it to.

Reliability in psychological measurement can have one of two different but related, meanings. The first meaning of reliability is *internal consistency*, that is the extent to which all parts of a measure are measuring the same thing. The second meaning of reliability is stability over time, that is the extent to which the measure is likely to change over time. You must be clear about which one of these definitions you are referring to when you use the word *reliability*.

INTERNAL CONSISTENCY

Crucial concept   *Internal consistency* concerns the extent to which different parts of a test are measuring the same thing.

To have internal consistency is important for all measures in psychology, but it is particularly important in the sort of tests which use a series of items (questions or statements) such as personality, ability or attitude tests.

We need to check the internal consistency of the set of items on the test. There are several ways to check the internal consistency. We will look at two here.

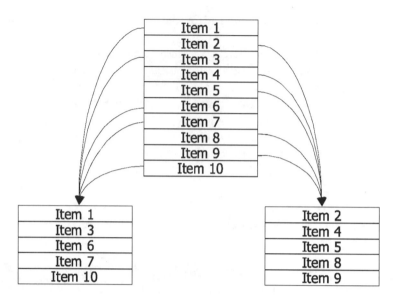

Figure 4.1: Calculating a split-half correlation. A test comprising ten items is randomly split into two tests, comprising five items each. The scores on the two tests are then correlated to give a split-half correlation.

Split-half correlation

One way of doing this is by calculating *a split-half correlation*. To do a split-half correlation, we take a test which has a number of items, and we randomly divide the items into two equal sized sets – this is shown in Figure 4.1. The next stage is to *correlate* the results of the two halves of the test. (A correlation is a measure of agreement between two sets of scores.) If the correlation is high, it means that people who score high on one set of items will also score highly on the other set of items, meaning that the scores are internally consistent. (See Chapter 8 for more information on correlations.)

Coefficient (Cronbach's) alpha

The problem, as you may have realised, with using a split-half correlation is that there are an awful lot of ways that we could split a set of items, and each of those will give a different answer. A better approach is to use something called *coefficient alpha*, or sometimes *Cronbach's alpha*, which was developed by Cronbach (1951). Coefficient alpha is the average of the correlations of all the possible ways of dividing the test into two sets. The values of the results of the calculation will range from 0 to 1. (There are several different interpretations of Cronbach's alpha, all of which are equally correct. You may well read about others in other texts.) Values of 0.7 and above are usually considered adequate values of coefficient alpha.

STABILITY OVER TIME

The second meaning of reliability is stability over time. When we say a measure is reliable, we mean that it is stable over time. If we measure people on an attitude test, and we measure them all three months later, unless something dramatic has happened in the meantime we would expect them all to have broadly similar attitude scores. If their scores had changed, it might suggest to us that the measure was not measuring a stable attitude at all, but instead had been measuring a transient mood, or something else that was easily changed by circumstances.

To find out if a measure is stable over time, you would present a group of participants with a measure, wait some period of time (in journal articles you will be able to find examples of people who have waited ten minutes, and people who have waited 15 years or more), and then present people with the same measure. You then see, using a correlation coefficient (see Chapter 8), the extent to which people's scores have changed.

You might find two problems. The first problem is that if you only wait a short period, people will be able to remember what they said last time, and will repeat what they said before – because they do not want you to think that they are inconsistent. The second problem is that if you wait too long, people really might actually have changed their attitude. So, if you then find that people have different scores, you don't know if this is because your measure is unreliable or it is reliably recording a change in attitude. For this reason, two weeks is considered a reasonable amount of time to wait between tests.

Validity of measures

> Crucial concept   The *validity* of a measure is the extent to which it measures what it is supposed to measure.

By assessing the reliability of a measure, we have ensured that our measure is a good measure. However, we have only ensured that it is a good measure of *something*. We have not examined whether it is a good measure of what we want it to actually measure. Whether an instrument measures what we want it to measure is called *validity*.

There are many different aspects of validity, and we will consider three: *construct validity, predictive validity* and *content validity*.

CONSTRUCT VALIDITY

The notion of construct validity was introduced by Cronbach and Meehl (1955). A construct is built in the minds of psychologists and does not exist in any concrete way, but it does exist in a theoretical way as an idea. Constructs are things like intelligence, anxiety, depression or thinking time. We know about them, we know what we are talking about when we talk about them, but it is hard to pin them down.

To establish the *construct validity* of a measure we would use our knowledge of the construct, and compare scores on our measure with other measure that are supposed to measure other aspects of the construct. High scorers on intelligence tests should also be high scorers on other tests which measure things related to intelligence, but they should not (necessarily) be high scorers on a test of extraversion.

PREDICTIVE VALIDITY

Some texts you may come across distinguish between predictive validity, criterion validity, and concurrent validity. However, as Nunnally and Bernstein (1994) point out, 'using different terms … implies that the *logic* and *procedures* of validation are different, which is not true' (page 94, italics in original). We will therefore consider all of these together.

To establish predictive validity we assess how well our measure relates to some external criterion. This external criterion can be a measure taken at the time or a measure taken considerably later.

Knowing what to select as the criterion can be a problem: sometimes the criterion is clearly defined, sometimes it is not.

A-levels are used as a criterion to establish whether a student will be allowed to enter university. We assume that good A-level results tell us that the student will do well at university. Are A-level results a valid way of predicting success at university? We can find out by comparing A-level results with university career results. Therefore, a suitable criterion for the predictive validity of A-levels is university success.

With many other tests, it is not so easy. A university may want to test the predictive validity of a test, which can give some idea of who is a good lecturer, but what is a good lecturer? If we were to ask a range of students, the head of department and the other lecturers, we would get a wide range of different answers.

CONTENT VALIDITY

Content validity requires us to use our knowledge of the content of a domain to assess the validity of a test or measure. A final year degree mark is a measure of a student's ability and knowledge in a particular subject. If the assessment contained only questions about research methods and statistics, it would not have content validity, because we know that psychology is about more than statistics. On the other hand, if your final mark contained no assessment related to research methods and statistics, it would not have content validity, because we know that research methods and statistics is an important component of psychology. We cannot assess content validity without some knowledge of the domain that we are trying to measure — if we didn't know that psychological knowledge included as a component knowledge of research methods and statistics we would not be able to assess the content validity of your final degree mark.

Section summary

In this section we have looked at reliability and validity. A measure is reliable if it measures something well. We looked at two different meanings of reliability: internal consistency and stability over time. Internal consistency is assessed using the split-half correlation or coefficient (Cronbach's) alpha. Stability over time is assessed using a test-retest correlation. We examined three aspects of validity: construct, predictive and content validity.

Section 4   Methods of data collection

What are you studying?

Finally, we get to the actual measurement process. In this section we will consider a range of different methods of measurement. Each of these methods is a different way of trying to find out about a person's mental processes.

We will now consider some of the methods of collecting data. Each of these methods may be used in conjunction with any of the experimental or non-experimental research methods discussed in Chapters 2 and 3. In psychology, we are always interested in what is happening inside people's brains. We want to be able to look inside their heads and find out what they know, and what they want, and what they believe. We can't look inside their heads directly, so instead we have to take a different approach.

The first method we could use is to ask them — we ask them what they know, and they tell us. Psychologists call this a self-report, carried out with an interview or questionnaire method. The second method we could use is to watch them and see what it is that they do. Psychologists call this the observational method. The final thing we could do is monitor their bodies for a biological response. Psychologists call these physiological methods.

Self-reports: questionnaires and interviews

> Crucial concept *Questionnaires* and *interviews* are usually about asking people questions to find out what they think about something, or know about an issue.

Self-report methods of data collection involve asking people questions. We can do this by using questionnaires (which are usually paper based) or by using interviews. There is something of a fuzzy line between these two methods – a telephone interview, for example, may be just a questionnaire done over the telephone.

In this section, we will have a look at some of the issues that arise when we use surveys or questionnaires – that is, when we ask people questions. Many of the issues that we will cover occur for both interview and questionnaire methods and so we consider them together. At the end of this section, we will compare the two methods, to help you decide which you should be carrying out.

Designing a good questionnaire or interview schedule is surprisingly difficult, and we will only look very briefly at some of the issues. If you are going to use a questionnaire or interview in a research project, you should be sure to thoroughly read some good information. A start would be Oppenheim (2000) or Fink (1995). In the section below, we look at just one of the problems in designing appropriate questions.

What should you ask?

Many polls in popular newspapers are of this type, but even polls with more serious aims can have the same problems. The Marie Stopes International organisation recently carried out a survey to find out about parental attitudes to children's sex education. For one part of the survey, parents responded on a six-point scale (from 'strongly agree' to 'strongly disagree'):

'I do not feel quipped with the necessary information.'

'I do not feel confident to talk about sex with my children.'

'I don't know where to start.'

If you wanted to carry out a similar survey to that carried out my Marie Stopes International, and you were of the opinion that parents did not need any outside help with sex education, would you have asked those questions? If not, what would you have asked?

Whose questions are more likely to get to the truth? Yours, or the original questions?

Observation

> Crucial concept Data collection through *observation* involves monitoring and systematically recording the behaviour of participants.

Observation is a very direct approach to collecting data. In a survey, we ask people what they do in different situations. In a way, we are saying 'Watch yourself and then tell us what you did' – thus a survey may be considered to be 'indirect observation'. Therefore, when we, the researchers, watch people to see what they do, we can call this 'direct observation'.

Students are often misled into thinking that observation is a tool only of social psychologists who are carrying out experiments in social settings, or of developmental psychologists who place one-way mirrors in nurseries. While observation certainly does include that type of research, you should realise that it covers a range of other areas of psychology.

Observations may also be used as the basis of surveys, or to back up and validate surveys. The supermarket Tesco sells a large number of pork pies, but in their surveys no one admitted to buying them. Observational research revealed that it was middle-aged men who bought them but did not want to admit in front of their wives that they ate pork pies.

Observational methods can be divided along two dimensions, formal vs casual, and participant vs non-participant. We will consider these in turn.

CASUAL vs FORMAL OBSERVATION

The relationship between casual and formal observational techniques is much like the relationship between unstructured and structured interviews described in the previous section.

Casual observation, like unstructured interviews, will often take place during the initial stages of a research project. The researcher will go to the situation looking to find the categories and behaviours that will be used later in the formal observation stage. In the first stage, the research-er may also be considering factors such as the best place to stand, or the least obtrusive way to dress.

When carrying out a formal observation the researcher will have a clear idea of what beha-viours they are looking for and how they will be recorded. It is common, especially in laboratory situations, to record information on video and then analyse it in more detail later.

PARTICIPANT vs NON-PARTICIPANT OBSERVATION

You can observe a group of people from two perspectives, either from outside the group or from within the group.

When researchers immerse themselves in a group so that they can observe behaviour from within the group they are known as *participant observers*. The participant observer has the advan-tage of being able to become completely involved with the group. The only way to really feel and understand what it is like to be a member of a group is to join that group. Sometimes this approach is the only way to observe the behaviour of a group. A famous example of this is Festin-ger, Riecken and Schacter (1956) who wanted to study a group of people who believed that the world was going to end on a particular day. They wanted to observe how they reacted when the world did not end, and joining the group was the only way that they could observe their beha-viour. The main disadvantage of this approach is that it is not possible to formally record all observations and behaviours – as soon as you start to take notes, the other members of the group will realise that something is amiss. A further disadvantage may be that you might have influenced the group by being there. You may try to do nothing, but by doing nothing, you may encourage others to do nothing – you don't know what would have happened if you weren't there.

In *non-participant observation*, the researcher remains separate from the group, and observes the group from a distance. This approach allows much more care to be taken in the observation of behaviours and the possibility of using video to record events so that they can be checked again for the accuracy of coding. The main disadvantage of this approach is that the individuals who are being observed may alter their behaviour because they are being observed.

THE RELIABILITY OF OBSERVATIONS

Researchers working with observational data must go to great lengths to ensure that their data are reliable. They must decide beforehand (often in the casual observation stage) precisely what they will be recording, and define these as accurately as possible. They can choose to describe very small units of behaviour (child X moved towards child Y; child Y smiled at child X) or larger units of behaviour (child X and child Y played together in the sandpit for 8 minutes).

Two types of reliability can be checked. They have confusing titles: *inter-observer reliability* and *intra-observer reliability*:

- *Inter-observer reliability* concerns the agreement between two separate observers, using the same scheme. If two observers with the same checklists and looking for the same behaviours, observe the same group of people, they should agree on what it is that they saw. If they disagree, then the checklist and the criterion should be revised.

- *Intra-observer reliability* concerns the agreement of observers with themselves. If you are observing a group over a long period, you might find that your criteria shift slightly. If possible, you should record the behaviours on video and then recheck earlier versions to ensure that you still agree with your earlier ratings.

ETHICAL ISSUES IN OBSERVATIONAL RESEARCH

We will cover ethical issues in much more detail in Chapter 5. However, it is worth mentioning ethical issues in this section to consider when it is acceptable to observe people without their knowledge.

The British Psychological Society Code of Conduct and Ethical Principles (BPS, 2000) states 'observational research is only acceptable where those observed would expect to be observed by strangers … particular account should be taken of … the possibility of intruding upon the privacy of individuals who, even while in a normally public space, may believe they are unobserved' (p. 12).

This means that if people are in a public space, surrounded by strangers, it is OK to observe their behaviour without their permission. An example of this would be examining whether people ate chips in the canteen. However, it is not acceptable to observe people just because they are in a public space – you would probably be unhappy about researchers observing your behaviour in a public toilet.

Physiological methods

> Crucial concept *Physiological measures* involve direct biological measurement of individuals.

The third method of data collection that we will examine is *physiological measurement*. This involves taking measurements of physiological, or biological, functioning:

- measures of heart rate, blood pressure and heart functioning;
- breathing and respiration;
- brain activity (measured using an electroencephalograph (EEG), magnetic resonance imaging (MRI) or computerised automated tomography (CAT);
- eye movements and responses;
- electrodermal response (also known as galvanic skin response), a measure of how much a person is sweating and therefore of how anxious they are;
- hormonal levels (can be measured directly through blood or indirectly, through saliva).

While most of these methods require special equipment and training, some of them are simple enough to be possible to carry them out in undergraduate projects. In addition, as we have said before, you can gain marks in practical reports by describing what you would have done, given enough time, expertise and equipment.

Section summary

In psychology, we want to know what people are thinking about. In this section we have examined three general ways of trying to find out. We can ask someone using either an interview or a questionnaire technique. We can observe them and look at their behaviour. We can take some sort of physiological measurement.

Further reading

For questionnaire design, the standard reference is the book *Questionnaire Design and Attitude Measurement* (Oppenheim, 2000). This has lots of useful information and advice to help you to write appropriate survey questions. Sage publishes a series of eight books, edited by Fink, called 'The Survey Kit':

- *A Survey Handbook*
- *How to Ask Survey Questions*
- *How to Conduct Self-Administered and Mail Surveys*
- *How to Conduct Interviews by Telephone and in Person*
- *How to Sample in Surveys*
- *How to Measure Survey Reliability and Validity*
- *How to Analyze Survey Data*
- *How to Report on Surveys.*

If you are interested in some of the special problems that arise in psychology, have a look at *People Studying People* by Rosnow and Rosenthal (published by Freeman). This is a clearly written book which contains lots of quite fun examples of curious and interesting research.

Books on psychological measurement often get quite heavy-going and mathematical so treat them with caution, but two good ones are *Psychological Testing* by Anastasi and Urbina and published by Prentice Hall, and *Psychometric Theory* by Nunnally and Bernstein and published by McGraw Hill (1994).

CHAPTER 5

ISSUES IN PSYCHOLOGICAL RESEARCH

Chapter summary

Studying this Chapter will help you to:

- Understand the sampling techniques that are used in psychological research.
- Evaluate sampling techniques in studies that you read about.
- Use appropriate sampling techniques in your studies.
- Understand your ethical responsibilities as a researcher.

Why do you need to know this?

In this chapter, we are looking at two 'loose ends'.

1. To carry out and evaluate research you need to understand issues in sampling – the methods used by researchers to find and recruit participants.

2. It is important that you have an understanding of ethical issues in research before you can carry out research. It is unlikely that you will be examined on this area directly, but you will need to show knowledge of the issues in your practical reports.

Crucial concepts

These are the key terms you will meet in this Chapter:

Cluster sampling	Random sampling
Ethical guidelines	Sampling
Ethics	Snowball sampling
Informed consent	Systematic sampling
Opportunity sampling	Volunteer sampling
Quota sampling	

Section I   Sampling

What are you studying?

Sampling is all about obtaining a sample from a population. In this section we will consider the approaches that can be used by psychologists to try to make sure that the sample is as representative as possible. At the end of this section, we will look at how sampling actually works in practice.

> Crucial concept   *Sampling* is the process of selecting research participants from the population.

In psychology, we want to answer questions about or we want to know about all five year olds, or all children at school in a particular area, or all people who work in similar jobs, or all pigeons. To find out accurately what we want to know, the ideal way would be to measure every individual in the population. Obviously this is not possible, so instead of measuring everybody we decide upon what is a manageable number of individuals to measure, and measure them instead.

The people (or pigeons) we are interested in are called the population; the people (or pigeons) we actually measure are called the sample. We hope to find a sample that is *representative* of the population. A representative sample will contain the same kinds of individuals and in the same proportions as the whole population.

In this section, we will look at some of the ways of selecting your sample from your population of interest. There is not necessarily only one correct method to use – different methods have different advantages and disadvantages. At the end of this section, we will discuss some of the techniques, in particular those that don't fit neatly into one of the standard categories.

Random sampling

> **Crucial concept** A *random sample* is a sample in which every member of the population has an equal chance of being selected and where selection of one member of the population does not alter the chances of any other person being selected.

Random sampling is the best method of selecting your sample from the population of interest. It is also the most difficult to achieve. Strictly speaking, statistical analyses are only valid if random samples are drawn. However, non-random samples, as long as they are not biased in any way, can be a reasonable alternative.

True random sampling is very rare, a perfection which can never be quite achieved. If someone says they have taken a random sample your first instinct should be not to believe them. If you write in a report that you took a random sample, you almost certainly did not. The *only* way to get a random sample of a population of people in the British Isles is to find out the name of every person in the population of interest (and if your population of interest is British adults, that is quite a large population), write all their names on individual pieces of paper (or do some computerised analogy), put all the pieces of paper into a hat and pick a sample out. If you don't follow a procedure like this one, you haven't taken a random sample. The same rules apply when you are sampling from some smaller population. Students sometimes write in their reports that they 'used a random sample of people in the canteen/street/laundrette/library'. However, they almost certainly did not.

> **Crucial tip** Always be careful when you use the word *random* in your practical reports. It has a specific meaning, and is often used to describe things which were not, strictly, random.

What looks like random sampling, but isn't

Each of the following examples contains a description of a method of sampling which appears as if it might be random, but is actually non-random. Why are each of these non-random?

- To obtain an random sample of Poppleton University students: wait outside a lecture theatre and pick every third person coming out.

- To obtain a random selection of adult residents in Uttoxeter: use the electoral register, put each name on a piece of paper and pick names from a hat.

- To obtain a random sample of residents of Camber: go to every third house in Hogwart and select one person from each house.

- To obtain a random sample of people who shop at Tesco: spend all Saturday at Tesco, rolling a dice very time someone goes past a checkout. If the dice comes up 6, select that person.

- To obtain a random sample of children in Hogwart's school: ask each teacher to write the names of all the children in their class on a piece of paper and select three names from each class from a hat.

Because obtaining a random sample is either unfeasible, or prohibitively expensive and time-consuming, a range of other techniques is used, which will (hopefully) also give a representative sample from our population.

Systematic sampling

> Crucial concept A *systematic sample* involves taking every *n*th individual from a list of names.

Systematic sampling, like random sampling, requires a list of all of the members of the population, but is easier to do. To take a systematic sample, you list all of the names of people in the population, and then decide upon a size of sample you would like. By dividing the number in the population by the number you want in your sample, you get a number which we will call *n*. If you take every *n*th name, you will get a systematic sample of the correct size. If, for example, you wanted to sample 150 children, from a school of 1,500, you would take every 10th name.

This is much easier than random sampling if you have a list of names. However, a list of names is not always available.

Quota sampling

> Crucial concept A *quota sample* is an attempt to make a sample representative by having the same proportions of different groups of people in the sample and in the population.

When you cannot take a random sample of the population, but you want to make your sample as representative as possible on a small number of variables, a *quota sample* can be used. You may know the proportions of people of different ages, salaries and sex in the population of interest. To make your sample as representative as possible, you want to reflect the proportions of the characteristics in the sample population.

Quota sampling at work

Scenario A: Thursday afternoon, nothing to do and wandering around the city centre, you see a market researcher. You amble by, looking like you didn't have a care in the world. They look through you. You stroll past again and are ignored. You try and do someone a favour, and they don't appreciate it.

Scenario B: Tuesday morning, job interview. Not sure of the exact location and a little anxious to make sure you're not late. See market research ahead – walk briskly ahead, looking concerned and busy, but they head towards you. 'Excuse me, could you spare a couple of minutes . . .' Do you *look* like you could spare a couple of minutes?

The market researcher is driven by a quota sample: they must get the correct number of each kind of person. If you are not the person they are looking for, they will ignore you. If you are, they can go home, if only they can get to interview you.

Cluster sampling

> **Crucial concept** A *cluster sample* takes a naturally occurring group.

Many populations occur in clusters, and these clusters often contain a range of types of individual. It may be a safe bet that each of those clusters contains a fair mixture of the kind of people who are to be found throughout the population, and it will be much easier to study one cluster than to take one sample from many different groups. Examples of clusters may be all children in a class, all GPs in Derbyshire, all members of a WI group, or all people drinking in a pub.

Opportunity sampling

> **Crucial concept** An *opportunity sample* is a sample of individuals who happen to be available.

An opportunity sample is obtained by asking members of the population of interest if they would take part in your research. At some point in your university career, students asking if you wouldn't mind filling in a questionnaire have probably accosted you. These students were asking you to be part of an *opportunity sample*.

Volunteer sampling

> **Crucial concept** *Volunteer sampling* involves selecting for research those people who put themselves forward.

You don't have to hang around very long anywhere psychology is taught before you see requests pinned to noticeboards for participants to take part in experiments. Sometimes people go into lectures to request that you take part in their research. Both of these methods of recruiting participants are examples of *volunteer sampling*. Psychologists may sometimes advertise in local newspapers or radio for participants. You may have come across Milgram's work on obedience to authority (Milgram, 1974/1997) – he used a newspaper advertisement to attract participants.

Comparing opportunity and volunteer sampling

Opportunity and volunteer sampling appear to be quite similar things, and some textbooks will put them together (calling them opportunity sampling). However, I think that it is worth considering them separately. The type of person who volunteers for a research project may be different from the type of person who would be willing to take part in a research project if asked.

Snowball sampling

> **Crucial concept** A *snowball sample* is used when a participant is used to introduce the researcher to further participants.

Snowball sampling is a very different sampling technique. It is a networking technique used when the population of interest is very difficult to get hold of, but it is likely that one member of the population of interest will know other members of the population who can be introduced to the researcher. Although the sampling technique is far from ideal, for some types of sample it is not possible to approach people or to advertise for individuals who would make suitable participants. Cusick (1998) studied drug use among prostitutes in Glasgow. To recruit her sample, she used a snowball technique. Cusick would interview one respondent, who would then introduce her to another potential respondent. In this way, Cusick was able to gain the trust of the respondents more quickly than if she had approached them individually without an introduction from another member of the group.

Sampling in practice

Sampling techniques are usually described in textbooks (including this one) as if only one technique is used at a time. In fact, in any one study, psychological researchers usually use a combination of techniques.

If you want to study children in a particular school, you cannot pick the children randomly from the school population. There are many hurdles to prevent you having random choice. First, you have to build up enough rapport with a school so that they will allow their pupils to participate in your research. If you are allowed access into a school, the headteacher may know which teachers are less busy and do not have something planned and are in a good mood that day. When you are given access to a class, you may be able to randomly select children from that class (but not the ones who are off sick).

As an example of this sort of combination research, Goldstein et al. (1993) wanted to sample children in schools in Britain. They used London as a cluster from which they selected schools randomly, and then classes randomly selected from those schools and children randomly from those classes.

> **Crucial tip**
>
> In your practical report you will often want to write that you used a specific type of sampling. Often, what you actually did, as we have seen, will not fit easily into one of the categories. If you find yourself in these circumstances, describe what you actually did and try to explain why you did it.

A final problem with sampling is that when you have selected participants, they may choose not to participate. If the participants refuse to answer your questions, they cease to be participants and you can't use them. (The way around this is to pay people to participate, but this gets expensive.)

Section summary

This section has considered sampling techniques that can be used to obtain a representative sample. We have looked at the 'textbook definitions' of random sampling, systematic sampling, quota sampling, cluster sampling, opportunity sampling, volunteer sampling and snowball sampling. We have also considered how the sampling technique that is actually used by psychologists varies from the textbook definitions.

Section 2   Ethical issues

What are you studying?

In this section we will consider ethical issues in psychological research – particularly the responsibilities that a researcher has with regard to the people who participate in their research. The overview is based on the British Psychological Society ethical guidelines for research with human participants.

> Crucial concept *Ethics* in psychological research is all about the moral duties of the psy-
> chologist. The main ethical responsibility of the researcher is to the
> people who take part in your research – the participants. However, a
> psychological researcher also has ethical responsibilities with respect to
> other researchers and to people in general.

Responsibilities to research participants

You should never forget that the people who take part in your research are doing *you* a favour. You should obviously do everything you can to protect them from physical harm, but you should also look after their psychological welfare. You should certainly make sure that they do not end up feeling foolish or silly. You should try to take up as little of their time as possible. You should be certain to keep everything they tell you confidential. You should not deceive them unless it is necessary.

Sometimes you may wish to replicate psychological research that you have read about. Sometimes the research that you wish to replicate may have involved the deception of participants, or putting participants under stress or in difficult or uncomfortable situations. If this research that you read about was carried out relatively recently, it would have been carefully scrutinised to ensure that it minimised any potential psychological harm to participants, that the stress imposed on the participants was absolutely necessary, that the research was carried out properly and that the findings of the research were worthwhile. When psychology students carry out research, they do so to learn how to carry out research. They do not carry out research to push forward the frontiers of science, and so the ethical criteria will be applied very strictly: you will not be justified as a student in carrying out deception or causing pain or stress.

You might have noticed that throughout this book that we usually use the word 'participant' rather than 'subject' for the people who take part in our research, although sometimes a term like 'respondent' is used to apply to people who, for example, fill in a questionnaire. We no longer use the term 'subject' because this term implies a passive individual who is 'experimented on' by a more knowing psychological 'experimenter'. The term participant is considered a more accurate word to reflect the role of a person who participates in your research as a favour to you.

Both the British Psychological Society (2000) and the American Psychological Association (1994) recommend the use of the word *participant*.

Ethical guidelines

Most countries have in place ethical guidelines for psychologists. The British Psychological Society (BPS) guidelines were most recently updated in January 2000, and are available from the BPS website (http://www.bps.org.uk).

The guidelines cover many areas in which psychologists may be involved, and include psychological research with humans and research with animals and research in areas of professional practice such as clinical psychology or occupational psychology.

In the next section, we will look at the guidelines relating to human participants in psychological research.

INFORMED CONSENT

> Crucial concept Participants give *informed consent* to take part in research when they fully
> understand the nature and purpose of the research.

Participants should give their consent to take part in research. This consent should be informed consent — it is not good enough to ask participants 'Will you take part in my study?' You should inform them, as fully as possible, what the study entails and why you are carrying it out. However, just because you have told them about the study does not mean that they understand. Participants should also be given the opportunity to ask questions about the study. It is especially important to inform them of anything that you suspect might influence their willingness to take part in the study.

DECEPTION

Deception is a difficult issue in psychological research. Much psychological research relies on deception — if people are aware that some aspect of them is being studied, they may behave differently than they would if they were not aware that this aspect of them was being studied. Since the researcher is interested in ordinary behaviour, there is a temptation to deceive so that the participants will not be tempted to 'bend' their behaviour. That said, no one likes to be lied to, and participants may be justifiably upset if it turns out that they were not told the truth about the study.

Deception comes in two flavours — omission and commission. Omission of information — not telling all — is usually easier to justify. Commission — that is deliberately saying something that you know to be untrue — is much more difficult to justify. The BPS guidelines state: 'Participants should never be deliberately misled without extremely strong scientific or medical justification.' As I have already stated, it is unlikely that *your* research project will be *that* important.

Often psychology students have the impression that participants should routinely be misled, or at least that they should not be informed of the true purpose of the study. However, such deception is often unnecessary and may do more harm than good. For example, if a student is carrying out a study on memory using an independent groups design (see Chapter 2) it can do very little harm to tell the participants that the study is looking at memory and that another group of participants will be given slightly different materials to learn — you are interested in seeing which type of material leads to better retention. Despite the fact that truth telling will not have an adverse effect on the results, students tend to choose not to tell participants what the research is about. Participants who are not informed of the true nature of the research may become suspicious and wonder what the research really is about. Participants may even fail to try hard enough to learn the material — because they will think that you have some ulterior motive and they will be looking for this instead.

DEBRIEFING

Debriefing is an important part of psychological research and is often considered too lightly by students. In the debrief you should ensure that participants are informed of the true nature of the study and you should also ensure that you send them away at least as happy (happier would be better, of course) as when they started, and that all of their questions are answered. Simply saying something like, 'Thanks, it was an experiment on memory' is not good enough. Sometimes students hand a piece of paper to the participant which explains the nature of the study. This is also not good enough.

To debrief your participants you should explain to each of them individually the nature of the study and say why you did what you did. You should ensure that they understand what you told them and you should give them the opportunity to ask any questions that they want answered. You should reassure them, if necessary, about any fears that they may have had. Some participants may be concerned that they performed badly or that they did not come out as 'normal'. If you send them away with a piece of paper, you will never discover that they have these beliefs, and you will not be able to give the needed reassurance.

Debriefing should not be treated as a chore that has to be done because the rules say so: it can be a very useful part of the experimental process. Sometimes in the course of debriefing, your participants may explain to you that they did not understand some part of the experimental procedure, or they may point out some flaw in your design that you were not aware of. (By using a debrief in this way, you are emphasising the fact that the participants take part in the research process, and that they are not 'subjects' whom you 'experiment on'.)

WITHDRAWAL FROM THE INVESTIGATION

At the start of the study, you should make sure that participants understand that they have the right not to take part in the experiment and have the right to withdraw at any point. Participants can also withdraw retrospectively: after debriefing, they can ask that their data and any recordings be destroyed.

You must distinguish between simply telling people that they have a right to withdraw and really giving people a right to withdraw. If you are testing your participants in a large group, there may be social pressure not to withdraw, particularly if they are forced to withdraw publicly. Saying 'If anyone doesn't want to take part, please put up your hand' may *look* as if it is giving your participants a right to withdraw, but is it?

CONFIDENTIALITY

Participants have a right to expect that any information that you collect on them is kept confidential. If you have sensitive data, you should ensure that participants' names are not recorded next to the data. The usual way to do this is to keep a paper record of names linked to code numbers. You can then separately keep a record of code numbers with the original data.

PROTECTION OF PARTICIPANTS

This section of the guidelines seems to be straightforward – protect your participants from psychological and physical harm. In fact, you may need to think hard about what might cause psychological stress.

It is not good enough to assume that a procedure will probably not cause stress: you must consider the types of things that *might* cause stress for some people and should therefore be avoided. You cannot, of course, eliminate all risk of causing stress, but you should go to all possible lengths to minimise this risk.

For instance, you should consider how people of different backgrounds, viewpoints or religions might view the research procedure. Many procedures that we might think harmless can be quite distressing for some participants.

In a study of problem-solving, you give participants a series of problems to solve, but some participants may find these problems to be very difficult, or become distressed that they are unable to solve the problems when they feel that they should be able to. Participants may also be worried that they were unable to solve the problems, and have therefore somehow 'failed' you or spoilt the study in some way. Your debrief needs to be sufficiently detailed to allay any fears that participants might have.

In a study of perceptions of taste you might blindfold participants and give them a liquorice allsort to eat. Liquorice allsorts may contain: gelatine (which is an animal product), which might offend vegetarians; milk, which people might be allergic to; and a mixture of meat product (gelatine) and milk product, which would be unacceptable to some Jewish people.

If you are using any type of equipment, you have a responsibility to ensure that it is safe and working correctly – most electrical equipment in universities will be subjected to a Portable Appliance Test (PAT), which ensures that it is electrically safe.

OBSERVATIONAL RESEARCH

In observational research, participants are often unaware that they are taking part as research participants. If the individuals have not given their consent, observational research should only take place in areas where the participants are in a public place and they would expect strangers to be able to observe them. If people are in a public place, but believe that they are in private and are not being observed, then observations should not take place.

Section summary

In this section, we have considered the ethical responsibilities that psychological researchers have towards their participants. The guidance is based on the British Psychological Society ethical guidelines for research with human participants, and covers six areas:

- Participants must give *informed consent* to take part in the research.
- Participants must not be *deceived*.
- Participants must be *fully debriefed*.
- Participants must have, and understand that they have, a *right to withdraw* at any time from the research.
- Participants must be *protected from physical or psychological harm*.
- Special consideration must be given to the protection of privacy of participants during *observational research*.

Further reading

For more information on ethics, see the British Psychological Society Code of Conduct, Ethical Principles and Guidelines, available on the Internet at http://www.bps.org.uk/documents/Code.pdf.

The US Government Office for Human Research Protections has an excellent and detailed guide to informed consent on the Internet at http://ohrp.osophs.dhhs.gov/humansubjects/guidance/ictips.htm.

For a nice short book on ethical issues, have a look at Mike Cardwell's book *Ethical Issues in Psychology* (published by Routledge). For a more in-depth discussion, and a longer book, see *Ethical Issues in Behavioral Research* by Allan Kimmel (published by Blackwell).

CHAPTER 6

DESCRIPTIVE
STATISTICS

Chapter summary

Studying this Chapter will help you to:

- Understand when to use different descriptive statistical techniques.
- Evaluate the use of descriptive statistics in research that you read about.

Why do you need to know this?

Everybody knows that there are 'lies, damn lies and statistics'. The point of this chapter is to show you the difference between lies and damn lies on the one hand and carefully analysed statistics on the other. If we were to play Monopoly together, when you did not know the rules and I were determined to win, you would be foolish to rely on me to find out the rules. 'Did I forget to tell you that if you land on Mayfair, but the other player owns Vine Street, you can't buy it?' It is better to find out the rules before you play the game. In the same way if you do not know the rules of statistics, someone who is attempting to bend the rules or someone who is not competent may take you in. This chapter will show you some of the rules of statistics.

Many students approach their statistics as if it is a mathematical problem. In a way, it is a maths problem, but it is not much of a maths problem. If you have a calculator, and can press the $+$, $-$, $\div$, $\sqrt{}$, and $=$ buttons, you are good enough at maths to do all of the statistics that you will be expected to do in your studies of psychology. If you are using a computer, the problems are much easier. You will need to do (almost) no maths at all to do the statistical analysis. The problem is that you will need to *think* about what you need to do, and this is much harder.

We will try to give algorithms that eliminate the need to make you think, but sometimes simple algorithms are not sufficient to find the answers to some questions and a bit of brainwork is necessary. There are times when there are differences of opinion between psychologists about how certain data should be presented – there is often more than one way to present data. Some researchers will also show preferences for or against methods. You need to be aware of the possibility of the biased researcher and be prepared to consider this bias when you analyse the work of others or plan your own.

Crucial tip	There is not necessarily a single correct way to present your data. However you present your data, someone could say that you should have presented it differently.

Crucial concepts

These are the key terms you will meet in this Chapter:

Dispersion	Mode
Distribution	Normal distribution
Histograms	Outliers
Interquartile range	Range
Kurtosis	Skew
Mean	Standard deviation
Median	Variance

Section I — Initial description of data

What are you studying?

In this section we will consider how you can describe the distribution of a set of data. We will look at some frequency tables and then frequency plots. We will examine the shape of distributions, particularly with reference to the normal distribution.

Descriptive data analysis is the use of techniques that take a set of raw scores and summarise them in a form that is more manageable. This chapter will show you several procedures that can be used to carry out descriptive data analysis.

Crucial tip   Descriptive statistics simply describe what you have found *in your sample*. They do not attempt to go beyond the data obtained, they make no predictions as to whether more results are likely to be similar if the research was to be replicated, and they do not explain what caused the result. Descriptive statistics show the results of a study in a way that can be easily understood.

A good place to start to describe your data is to look at the frequencies of different scores. How often does a particular value come up?

One way of summarising data is presented in Table 6.1. This shows the number of times each score appears. This table shows the results correctly, but how long does it take you to see what the most common score is? And the second most common score? The table contains correct information, but it is not in a clear and easy to read form. The information can be represented instead in a histogram.

Value (score)	Frequency (number of pupils achieving that score)
0	5
1	3
2	8
3	9
4	4
5	8
6	8
7	3
8	1
9	1

Table 6.1: Frequency table.

Crucial concept   *Histograms* show the frequency of particular numbers appearing in a dataset.

Histograms show the shape of a distribution (more on this later) and outliers (more on this later). A histogram can be drawn with bars, or with a line joining up the points. Along the x (horizontal) axis you will find the possible scores. On the y (vertical) axis you will find the number of people who have that score.

This second way of presenting the same information is shown in Figure 6.1. Notice now that, from the graph in Figure 6.1, it is much quicker and easier to answer questions such as 'What is the most common score?' (Three is the most common score since nine pupils achieved it.)

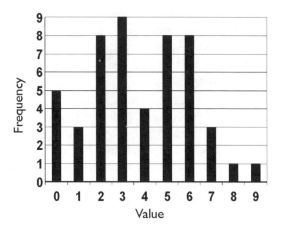

Figure 6.1: Histogram using bars of data shown in Table 6.1.

> **Crucial tip**   What is the difference between a histogram and a bar chart? A histogram (if drawn with bars) is a special kind of bar chart. A bar chart may show anything on the x-axis or on the y-axis. A histogram always shows values on the x-axis and frequency on the y-axis; in addition the values on the x-axis of a histogram represent a scale and should be placed to represent the scale.

Histograms and distributions

When a histogram is plotted, you can see the 'shape' of the distribution of the variable (i.e. how many had low scores, how many in the middle, how many high scores). Because they give a visual representation of the *shape* of a distribution, histograms are very important in data analysis.

> **Crucial concept**   Strictly speaking a *distribution* is a mathematical function that describes the probability of any score occurring. Less strictly speaking, you can think of a **distribution** as the shape of a curve on a histogram.

One of the most common distributions is the *normal distribution* (also known as the *Gaussian distribution*) illustrated in Figure 6.2. A very large number of naturally occurring variables are normally distributed. A large number of statistical tests make the assumption that the data form a normal distribution.

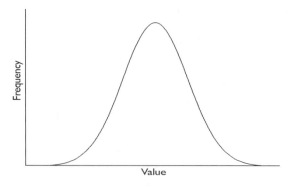

Figure 6.2. A normal distribution.

> Crucial concept   A *normal distribution* is *symmetrical*, and *bell shaped*. It curves outwards at the top, and then inwards nearer the bottom, the *tails* getting thinner and thinner. Figure 6.2 shows a *perfect* normal distribution.

Your actual data will never form a perfect normal distribution, but you can expect that it will be close: if the distribution formed by your data is symmetrical, and approximately bell-shaped, then you have something close to a normal distribution.

Departing from normality

WRONG SHAPE

There are two ways in which the shape of a distribution can fail to be *normal*: it can have skew (asymmetry) or kurtosis (being too tall or too flat to be considered a bell curve).

Skew

> Crucial concept   A distribution is *skewed* if it is not symmetrical. (Recall that a normal distribution is symmetrical.)

Figures 6.3 and 6.4 both show distributions that are non-symmetrical, and are therefore said to be *skewed*. Figure 6.3 shows *positive skew* (the curve rises rapidly, and then drops off slowly) and Figure 6.4 shows *negative skew* (the points rise slowly, and then decrease quickly).

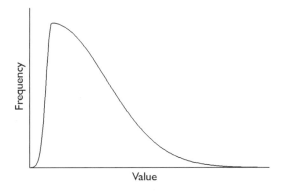

Figure 6.3: Histogram showing positively skewed distribution.

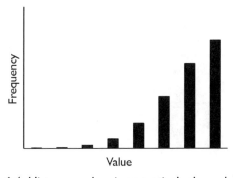

Figure 6.4: Histogram showing negatively skewed distribution.

> **Crucial tip**   Negative skew starts flat, like a minus sign. Positive skew starts going up, like part of a plus sign.

Skew, as we shall see later on, has some serious implications for some types of data analysis.

Kurtosis

> **Crucial concept**   A distribution that is non-normal because it is too flat or too peaked is described as *kurtosed*.

Kurtosis is a much trickier issue than skew: it can be harder to work out why it has occurred, and it can be harder to know what to do about it. If you find that the description of kurtosis is confusing, you should be reassured that many researchers and even textbook authors find that they are confused by kurtosis (DeCarlo, 1997). Luckily for us, the issue of kurtosis is much less serious than the issue of skew in data analysis.

Like skew, kurtosis can be either positive or negative. Positive kurtosis occurs when the ends (or tails) of the distribution contain too many people. This makes the distribution wider and more peaked than a normal distribution.

The second way a distribution can be kurtosed is negatively. If a distribution is negatively kurtosed, there are not enough points in the tails of the distribution. This causes confusion because it appears that the distribution is too flat, as if someone has sat on it and pushed too many people to the tails – this isn't the case, it is more like the tails have been chopped off the distribution. If the distribution is flat, then it is negatively kurtosed. In an extreme case, the distribution may have two separate peaks – this is called a bimodal distribution.

OUTLIERS

> **Crucial concept**   Even when your distribution is approximately normal, you may find that there are a small number of data points that lie outside the main part of the distribution. These points are called *outliers*.

Outliers are usually easy to spot on a histogram such as the one in Figure 6.5. The data seem to be normally distributed, but there is just one pesky point out there on the right-hand side.

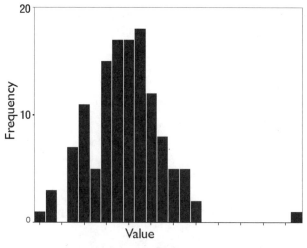

Figure 6.5. A normal distribution with an outlier.

Outliers are easy to spot, but deciding what to do with them can be much trickier. If you have an outlier, you need to do some checking to decide what you should do about it.

First, you should see if you have made an error in entering your data. Data entry errors are the most common cause of outliers. Look for numbers that should not be there. If the maximum score on a test is 10, and someone has scored 66, then you have made an error.[1]

If you don't find an entry error, look for a measurement error. You should now check that any measurement that you took was done correctly. Did a piece of equipment malfunction?

Obviously, if you find an error, you correct it if you can. If you cannot find an error, you must conclude that the data point is a 'real' data point. If it was a measure of reaction time, did the participant sneeze or yawn? Did they understand the instructions? Is there something unusual about them that means that they should not have been measured? If any of these are the case, you should try to correct the error in some way and enter the correct value – if you can. If you cannot find the correct value, you should delete the data point. This may seem like cheating – you are throwing away a valid data point. However, you need to think about the underlying psychological process that generated the data point. If the participant who generated that reaction time did it because they sneezed, the psychological process was not the same and you should not be interested in that process.

If you cannot eliminate any of these errors and are convinced that you have a genuine measurement, then you have a dilemma. Your first option is to eliminate the point, and carry on with your analysis. If you eliminate the point, you will analyse your data well, but you will not analyse *all* of your data. Alternatively, you can keep the data point and analyse all of your data, but, as we will see in the next chapters, keeping the outlier in means that your distribution will not be normal and therefore the analysis you do will not be correct – and therefore you will analyse your data badly. Not much of a choice. (Sorry.)

Section summary

When exploring your data, the first thing you should look at is the distribution of the data. This is done most easily using a histogram (frequency plot). The histogram will show you if the data are normally distributed. If they are not normally distributed, they may be non-formal because the data form the wrong shape or because there is a small number of outliers.

If the data form the wrong shaped distribution, the shape of the distribution may be skewed (non-symmetrical) or kurtosed (too flat or too peaked). Skew is more serious than kurtosis. Outliers might be errors. If they are errors, they should be fixed; if they are not errors, they should probably be removed.

Section 2   Measures of central tendency

What are you studying?
This section is all about averages – or rather measures of central tendency, as the word average is ambiguous and is better avoided. We look at three different meanings of the word average: the mean, the median and the mode, and we consider when it is appropriate to use each of these measures.

---

[1] Alternatively your participants may have given you the wrong information. If someone writes 784 in the 'age' slot, they will be an outlier, or (as I once saw a student write) an 'outright liar'.

To use the word 'average' is ambiguous. In common usage, *average* refers only to what is technically know as the *arithmetic mean*, whereas in statistics, average can refer to any of several measures of central tendency. Therefore this book will largely avoid the word 'average', and whenever you hear someone else use the word 'average', you should always think about which average they mean.

The purpose of measuring central tendency is to describe a group of individual scores with a single measurement. The value we use to describe the group will be the single value that we consider to be most representative of all the individual scores.

Figure 6.6. The 'average' family
with 1.9 children.

Central scores are the most representative so (using everyday language) the goal of central tendency is to find the 'average' or 'typical' score. This average value can then be used to provide a simple description of the entire population or sample. Be careful not to say that this is the score of the average person though, or you find yourself saying things like 'The average family has 1.9 children.' Instead, you should say 'The mean number of children per family is 1.9.'

Measures of central tendency are useful for making comparisons between groups of individuals or between sets of figures. They reduce a large number of measurements to a single figure, and thus make comparisons easy. The mean temperature in Central England in July from 1961 to 1990 was 16.1 degrees. Over the same period in September it was 13.6 degrees. We have summarised a lot of information in two numbers, and we can say that it is likely to be warmer in July than September in Central England.

Unfortunately, there is no single, standard procedure for determining central tendency. The problem is that no single measure will always produce a typical, representative value in every situation. Therefore we will consider three different ways to measure central tendency: the mean, the median and the mode. These three statistical measures are computed differently and have different characteristics. To decide which of these is best for any particular distribution, you should keep in mind that the general purpose of central tendency is to find the single most representative score.

Mean

Crucial concept   To calculate the *mean*, you sum (add up) each individual score and divide by the number of scores.

The mean is what we all think of as the average. Strictly speaking, it is called the arithmetic mean because there are other types of mean (although you are very unlikely to come across one).

As you probably know, adding up all of the scores and dividing the total by the number of individual scores gives the mean. This is written in equation form as shown below. The scores of whatever we have measured, whether it is *temperature*, *IQ* or *time taken to solve a problem*, we will now refer to as x. In statistical formulae, x represents all the separate values in a particular distribution. The mean of the variable x is written as $\bar{x}$, and pronounced 'x-bar'. Even if you know how to calculate the mean, have a look at the equation below so that you get used to the format.

$$\bar{x} = \frac{\Sigma x}{N}$$

In this equation the Greek letter Σ, or sigma, means 'add up'. So this equation says 'add up x' (where x is a set of scores) and 'divide by N' (where N is the number of scores in x).

ASSUMPTIONS

We often need to make assumptions in everyday life; in the UK, we assume that everyone else will drive on the left-hand side of the road. We assume that when we press a light switch, the light will come on. We assume that if we do enough work and understand enough then we will pass our exams. We make similar assumptions in statistics: we assume, often, that the data will be distributed normally. If the distribution we are dealing with is not normal, these assumptions are wrong (statisticians usually say *violated*), and it follows that our statistical analysis will be wrong.

However, while our assumptions will usually be *broadly* correct, they will never be *exactly* correct. People sometimes drive on the wrong side of the road (when parking, for example) but most of the time we manage not to crash into them. If people drove on the wrong side of the road a lot, we would have more serious problems.

Similarly, if our assumptions about data are wrong, but not too wrong, we need to be a little bit aware that our statistics will not be perfectly correct, but as long as the assumptions are not violated to any *great* extent, we will be able to find some useful results from our analysis.

The mean is a useful statistic only if:

1. The distribution of your data is symmetrical – not too much skew, and no outliers;

2. The data are measured at the interval or ratio level. We saw in Chapter 6 that data can be measured at a number of levels. It would not be sensible to say that half of the people were wearing blue shoes and half of the people were wearing yellow shoes, and that therefore the mean shoe colour was green.

The mean, the median and lying with statistics

The mean is sensitive to skew and can be distorted if there is skew in the data. This is a good example of when people can lie with statistics (but only to people who do not understand statistics).

In most societies, pay is not normally distributed – it is positively skewed. Most people earn a small to moderate amount of money, a smaller number of people earn a lot of money, and a very small number of people earn a very substantial amount of money.

The mean amount of money that people earn can increase just by increasing the amount of money that a small number of people earn. If 99 people earn £10,000 per year, and one person earns £1,000,000 per year, the mean amount of money earned is £19,900.

If I double the pay of the one person who earns £1,000,000 per year, then the mean pay becomes £29,900. I can say, 'Thanks to me, the average person has had a pay rise of over 50%', although 99% of people have had no extra cash.

Median

Crucial concept   The *median* is the central score – the one in the middle.

The median is the second most common measure of central tendency. It is the middle score in a set of scores. The median is useful when the mean is not valid, either because the data are not symmetrically or normally distributed or because the data are measured at an ordinal level.

If the scores are placed in ascending order of size from the smallest to the largest, the median is the middle one. To find the median when then there is an odd number of scores in the distribution, halve the number of scores and then take the next whole number up and that will be the ordinal number of the median. For example, suppose there are 29 scores: sort the scores into ascending order (from the lowest to the highest), half of 29 is 14.5, round up to 15. The median is the fifteenth score.

If there is an even number of scores, the median is the mean of the two middle scores. If there are 18 scores, the median will be the number halfway between the ninth and the tenth scores.

Mode

> Crucial concept   The *mode* is the most common value.

The final measure of central tendency is the mode. We need to know what it is although it is rarely reported in psychological research. The definition of the *mode* is that it is the most frequent score in the distribution or the most common observation among a group of scores (you could think of it as the most 'fashionable' score). The mode is the only measure of central tendency appropriate for nominal data.

It is usually not very useful to report the mode. If I report that the modal (i.e. most common) shoe colour among a group was black, this tells you very little. Was everyone wearing black shoes? Were there three people wearing black shoes, and two people wearing shoes of every other colour?

ORDINAL DATA

When data are measured on an ordinal scale (see Chapter 4), we have to consider carefully whether to use the mean or the median, or even the mode. Opinions differ between psychologists, and so I have to be careful about what advice to give. There is nothing wrong with this difference in styles: Abelson (1995) defines four styles of data presentation: stuffy, brash, liberal and conservative, and you need to choose your style according to the demands of the audience.

The problem is that there is a very fuzzy line between what could *definitely* be called ordinal data, and what could *definitely* be called interval data. Some (very strict) psychologists would argue that the scales used with things like tests for IQ, personality and attitudes must be ordinal scales and the data produced must be considered to be ordinal data. The majority would argue that these can be considered interval data and therefore it is OK to use the mean. In most psychological journals, you will find that most researchers most of the time treat their data as interval data. (Note that treating your data *as if* they were measured on an interval scale is not the same as saying that your data *are* measured on an interval scale. You know the data are not interval, but you also know that it will probably do no harm to treat them as if they were interval.)

Section summary

The wood 'average' means three different things and should therefore be avoided. The mean is the average as we usually think of it. The median is the middle score and is the most common score. The mean should be used with interval data when the data are symmetrically (normally) distributed. The median should be used with skewed distributions or ordinal data. The mode should usually be used with nominal (categorical) data.

If the distribution of your data is skewed, the mean will be pulled in the direction of the skew. It is sometimes difficult to decide whether the data are measured on an ordinal scale and the median should be used, or whether the scale is an interval scale and the mean should be used. You choose the style of your presentation to fit in with the expectations of your audience.

Section 3 — Measures of dispersion

What are you studying?

In this section we consider a second type of summary statistic that can be used to describe data: a measure of dispersion, or spread. We first look at why measures of dispersion are important – it can be difficult to interpret a measure of average without a measure of dispersion. Then we investigate three different measures of dispersion: the range, the interquartile range and the standard deviation.

> **Crucial concept** — *Dispersion* is the degree of spread in a variable – it describes the distance from the average. When describing a variable it is vital to describe the central tendency, but the central tendency does not mean a lot without a measure of dispersion or spread.

An experiment was done to examine the effects of a mind-enhancing drug on memory performance. Participants in an experimental group were given a small dose of the drug before taking a memory test; participants in the control group were given a placebo before taking part in the test.

The results were as shown in Table 6.2. Look at the table and decide: did the drug have an effect on memory? How much of an effect was it?

Group	Mean score
Control (placebo)	70
Experimental (drug)	80

Table 6.2: Mean scores in memory experiment.

You can answer the first question – yes, the drug seemed to have an effect on memory, because the group that took the drug did better than the control group. The second question – how much of an effect was it? – you cannot answer because I haven't given you any information about the spread, or the dispersion, of the scores.

Have a look at Figures 6.7 and 6.8. The mean of the scores displayed on each graph are the same, but the graphs look very different because the spread, or dispersion, of the scores is very different in each of the graphs.

What this shows is that it is very hard to interpret a measure of central tendency without a measure of dispersion. The results of a measure of central tendency can be meaningless – or worse misleading – unless we also have a measure of dispersion.

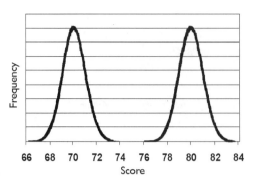

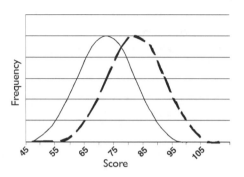

Figure 6.7: Experimental group (drug) mean = 80, control group (placebo) mean = 70. When the dispersion is very small, this is a very large difference between the two groups. If you knew what someone's score was, you would know which group they were in.

Figure 6.8: Experimental group mean = 80, control group mean = 70. When the dispersion is moderate, the same size difference between the two groups is harder to distinguish. If you knew what someone's score was, you could make a guess at which group a certain score belonged in, but you would not know for sure.

We will now look at three different measures of dispersion: the range, the interquartile range and the standard deviation.

Range

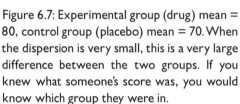

Crucial concept The *range* is the distance from the highest score to the lowest score.

The range is the simplest measure of dispersion. It is simply the distance between the highest score and the lowest score. It can be expressed as a single number, or as the highest and lowest scores.

We will find the range of the variable x which consists of eight scores: 4, 11, 17, 12, 3, 15, 10, 28.

To find the range in the above example, we identify the lowest value (which is 2), and the highest value (which is 17).

Sometimes the range is expressed as a single figure, calculated as:

$$Range = Highest value - Lowest value$$
$$= 17 - 2$$
$$= 15$$

Sometimes it is expressed as the range of scores: 'the range was 2 to 17'.

PROBLEMS WITH THE RANGE

The range suffers from one huge problem: it is massively affected by outliers. If one person gets a strange score, the range is highly distorted, and two dispersions that are actually very similar are suddenly made to appear very different – because one of them has an outlier. Because of this distorting effect of outliers, *range* is very rarely used in psychological research. It is most commonly used to describe some aspect of a sample that does not need to be summarised with any degree of accuracy. For example 'the ages of the participants ranged from 18 to 48' or 'class sizes ranged from 23 to 36'.

Interquartile range

The *interquartile range* is the range of the central 50% of a distribution. It is associated with the median.

The interquartile range (IQR) is used with ordinal data and with non-normal distributions. It is often used in conjunction with the median and is very similar to the median.

To find the interquartile range the scores are placed in rank order and counted. The halfway point is the median (as we saw previously). The IQR is the distance between the quarter and three-quarters distance points (see Figure 6.9).

Unlike the range, the IQR does not go to the ends of the scales and is therefore not affected by outliers. It is also not greatly affected by skew and kurtosis. The IQR is very similar to the median, and is usually used in conjunction with the median.

You might come across the semi-interquartile range. This is the interquartile range divided by 2, that is, it is half the interquartile range.

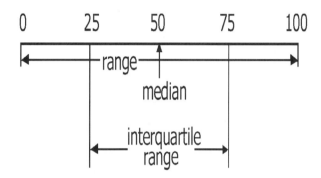

Figure 6.9: The median, the range and the interquartile range.

The standard deviation and the variance

> Crucial concept The *standard deviation* is a measure of the width of a normal distribution.

Finally, we shall look at the standard deviation (s) and the variance (s^2). The standard deviation and the variance are very closely related – the variance is simply the square of the standard deviation (i.e. the standard deviation multiplied by itself). The standard deviation is a measure of dispersion which (like the mean) takes all of the values in the dataset into account when it is calculated. It is also like the mean in that we must assume that we have a normal distribution before it is reasonable to use it.

> Crucial concept The *variance* is the square of the standard deviation.

There is an additional problem with the standard deviation – it comes in two different 'flavours'. What we usually talk about, when talking about the standard deviation and the variance, are the *sample* standard deviation (s) and the *sample* variance (s^2). You might also come across the *population* standard deviation, which is represented by the Greek letter σ (sigma) and the population variance (σ^2).

THE STANDARD DEVIATION AND THE NORMAL DISTRIBUTION

The standard deviation is a very useful statistical tool, particularly when combined with a normal distribution. In a normal distribution, we can express any value in terms of its distance from the mean in standard deviation units – this is called a z-score or a standardised score. To convert a value to a z-score, we subtract the mean and divide by the standard deviation.

Table 6.3 shows the original scores and the z-scores of values from a distribution where we know the mean to be 100 and the standard deviation to be 10. The original value of 100 is equal to the mean and so has a z-score of zero. The value 120 is 2 SDs above the mean, and so has a z-score of 2.0, etc.

Original score	z-score
100	0.0
120	2.0
80	−2.0
164	6.4
48	−5.2

Table 6.3: Original scores and z-scores from a distribution
where mean = 100 and SD = 10.

One advantage of z-scores over raw scores is that if we know (or can assume) that the original variable has a normal distribution, we know how often scores in different ranges will occur. For example, we know, in a normal distribution, that half of the scores will be above the mean and half of the scores will be below the mean. This means that if I have a z-score of 0.0, you know that half of the people in the sample will have a higher score than me and half of the sample will have a lower score than me.

We can consult tables, or use a computer, to find out how many people will score higher or lower than a particular value. Some of those values are shown in Figure 6.10.

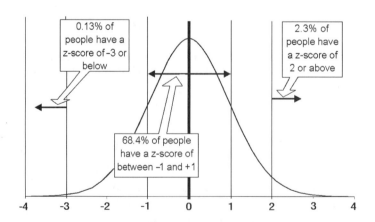

Figure 6.10: A normal distribution showing percentage of people who obtain different scores, expressed in terms of z-scores.

Section summary

Measures of central tendency should always be accompanied by a measure of dispersion as they cannot be interpreted without one. There are three measures of dispersion: the range, which is not used very often, the interquartile range, which should be used with the median, and the standard deviation, which should be used with the mean. The variance is another measure of dispersion, but is the square of the standard deviation.

Further reading

It is difficult to cover descriptive statistical analysis without getting a little bit, well, for want of a better word, dull. Huff's book *How to Lie with Statistics* (Penguin) gets around this problem in an original way – it looks at how you should not use descriptive statistics if you want to get your point across, and how other people might use descriptive statistics to disguise the nature of their data. Another book which takes an interesting approach is *Elements of Graph Design* by Kosslyn. Kosslyn is a cognitive psychologist who has carried out research on mental imagery and visualisation processes. In this book he takes the principles that have come from research in this area and applies it to graphs.

CHAPTER 7

WHAT ARE INFERENTIAL STATISTICS?

Chapter summary

Studying this Chapter will help you to:

- Understand the basis of statistical significance.
- Use the results of a significance test to make judgements about a hypothesis.
- Understand the factors that effect errors in statistical significance.

How will you be assessed on this?

You are unlikely to be assessed directly on this material. But you need to understand the material that is presented in this chapter if you want to have a thorough grasp of the information in the next chapter, and to have a better understanding of the way that inferential statistics are used in psychological research. This understanding will help you when it comes to evaluating research that you read about, and research that you carry out yourself. I should warn you that the material in this chapter is quite difficult, and it is possible to survive without a good grasp of this chapter.

Crucial concepts

These are the key terms you will meet in this Chapter:

Inference	Two-tailed hypothesis
One-tailed hypothesis	Type I error
Probability	Type II error

Section I — What are inferential statistics?

What are you studying?

In this section, we introduce some of the ideas involved in inferential statistics. We will have a look at probability, and see what is meant by probability, because this is the foundation of inferential statistics. Then we look at statistical significance and see how statistical significance relates to the null hypothesis which we looked at in Chapter I.

In the last chapter, we looked at descriptive, statistical analysis. We use exploratory data analysis to explore and describe the data that we have collected, using measures of central tendency (such as the mean), dispersion (such as the standard deviation) and appropriate graphs. If we were only interested in the people that we studied, our sample, then they would constitute our whole population. We would not need or want to do any inferential statistics – we could stop there. However, we are interested in much more than just our sample – we want to be able to generalise our sample to the population from which we obtained our sample.

In other words, we want to know if the results that we found in our sample are likely to be true in the population. This process is called *inferring*.

> Crucial concept   To *infer* is to derive a conclusion from facts – if we see smoke, we can infer that there is a fire.

Of course, we can never be sure that there is a fire – there may be a smoke-making machine, or we may have seen steam and mistaken it for smoke. Similarly, in psychological research we can never know for sure that a result for the sample will also be true for the population. We can never know absolutely for sure, but we can make an educated guess about whether the sample result will be true of the population we were sampling, and this is where we need inferential statistics.

Inferential statistical analysis is all about probability. We cannot, as mentioned above, speak in terms of **absolute** truth or falsehood when we are speaking about the natural world. Instead, we can say that something is likely to be true, or probably true. We can also say that something is likely to be false, or that it is probably false.

Therefore, when you use inferential statistics, you are talking about the likelihood of things – how likely they are to happen. To do this, we need to understand a little bit about probability theory.

A bit on probability

There are many different ways of expressing a probability: people tend to say things like '10%' or '1 in 10' chance.

> Crucial concept In statistics, *probabilities* are expressed as numbers between 0 and 1: 10% or 1 in 10 chance would be expressed as a probability of 0.1.

It is a good idea to get used to understanding the relationship between these different ways of saying the same thing. As a practice, have a go at filling in the blanks in the following table (answers over the page). It is not a good idea to express probabilities in terms of odds, e.g. 10 to 1, because this can be confusing and ambiguous (see Note for gamblers).

Probability	Percentage	Proportion
0.25	25%	¼
0.4		⅖
	80%	
0.75		
		⁷⁄₁₀

Note for gamblers

Betting shops tend to express the probability of an event in terms of odds. This makes it easy to work out how much you will be paid but can be confusing in terms of probabilities.

What are the odds of a horse winning, which has a probability of winning of 0.25 (i.e. one in four)?

If you said 4:1, you were wrong. The answer is 3:1. This is because when you say '1 in 4' you mean that in four races, the horse will win once. The betting shop says that it will lose three races and win one. The same thing, but rather a different way of putting it.

If an event has a probability of 0, *it will not happen*. No matter what. If an event has a probability of 1, *it will happen*. No matter what. An event cannot have a probability less than 0 or greater than 1.

The probability of an event occurring is written as p(event). It is calculated using:

$$p(event) = \frac{\text{Number of events which satisfy criterion}}{\text{Total number of events}}$$

When it comes to tossing a coin, there is one event that satisfies our outcome (heads) and one that does not (tails), making two possible events. We know that the probability of tossing a coin and it landing heads is equal to 0.5 or 1/2 because heads is one outcome out of two possible outcomes.

This is where the tricky bit starts …

Statistical significance

> Crucial concept A *statistically significant* result is a result which would be unlikely to occur if the null hypothesis were correct.

Some words used in everyday life have a specific technical meaning in psychology. One of the most common of these is the word *significant*.

When we have carried out a study and collected our data, we analyse the data initially using the descriptive statistical techniques that were discussed in Chapter 7.

We may want to know whether these results are generally true or whether we have just been lucky: we want to know if we can *generalise* these results to the population. What we want to know is, are our results *statistically significant*. Before we go on to discuss this, there are two points to note about statistical significance.

- First, people shorten this phrase and just write 'significant' when they mean 'statistically significant'. Doing this is slightly dangerous, because results may be 'significant' without being 'statistically significant', or results may be 'insignificant' despite being 'statistically significant'.[1]

- Second, a result that is not statistically significant is not 'insignificant', it is either non-significant or, better, it is 'not statistically significant'.

STATISTICAL SIGNIFICANCE AND THE NULL HYPOTHESIS

We looked at hypotheses in Chapter 1 when we considered the scientific method. We will have a quick look again in this section, but if you have not read Chapter 2, you might find it easier if you read the relevant section before tackling this one.

When psychologists want to find something out, they set up a hypothesis which reflects their theory, and a corresponding null hypothesis which contradicts their theory and can be tested.

Let's say that you decide to study the hypothesis 'Psychology students who work harder at statistics have fuller, happier lives'.

You sample a group of psychology students (see Chapter 6 for a discussion of how you might do this) and divide them into two groups. The first group, the High Work Group, spends more than five hours per week working on their statistics. The second, the Low Work Group spends less than five hours per week working on statistics. You then measure how full and happy the students' lives are.

Using the descriptive techniques and graphs described in Chapter 7, you can compare the two groups. Let's say your findings are the statistics shown in Table 7.1. They tell us that the students in our sample who spent more time working on statistics had fuller and happier lives (according to our measure). However, we are not just interested in our sample – if our results are only true for our sample, that is not much of a result. We want to know if this result is *generally* true – is it true for the population that we drew our sample from?

---

[1] A television programme I saw recently had a reporter interviewing a scientist who had carried out some work on BSE (mad cow disease). The reporter said, 'Was this result significant?' The scientist replied, 'Oh yes.' I am not sure, but I suspect that they did not mean the same thing when they said 'significant'.

	Mean score	SD	N
High Work Group	20.0	10.0	25
Low Work Group	10.0	10.0	10

Table 7.1: Mean and SD fullness and happiness of life scores
of students in high and low work group.

To find out if this result will be likely to be true in the population, you use inferential statistics. You carry out a statistical test (more on that later on and in the next chapter). In this case you would carry out a t-test (don't worry about why for now), and you would find that $t = 5.34$.

More tricky bits . . .

This result (t) does not mean anything to you. Students often don't like that idea – they insist that it must mean something and that they should understand what it means. You shouldn't and you almost certainly won't.

Other people (again, those people who are cleverer than we are) have looked at the distribution of t under the null hypothesis. They have calculated how likely it is different values of t will occur if the null hypothesis is correct. We don't need to understand what they did or how they did it. We want to know how likely it is that values of t as large as 5.34 (our t score) will appear if the null hypothesis is true. The t distribution looks a little like the normal distribution, but unlike the normal distribution, which is always the same shape, the shape of the t distribution depends on something called the degrees of freedom (df), which we will encounter later on.

You can find the associated p-value either by looking it up in a table or using a computer. It is likely that the computer will also tell you the probability associated with values of t that large.

End of tricky part.

When you have found the value of t, you will find the associated probability. This will tell you the probability of getting a value of t that large, *if the null hypothesis is correct*. As we will see later on, this is not the same thing as the probability of the null hypothesis being correct. The *probability value* associated with the statistical test we carried out is very small – less than 0.0001. I know this probability from looking it up in a book with the appropriate table in it, or because the computer program that I used to calculate t also told me the probability associated with it.

Before we do the study, we should decide on a probability that will be low enough for us to reject the null hypothesis. This value is known as alpha (the Greek equivalent of the letter *a*, written as α. If the probability is below alpha – usually less than 0.05 – then we can reject the null

Answers

Probability	Percentage	Proportion
0.25	25%	1/4
0.40	40%	2/5
0.80	80%	4/5
0.75	75%	3/4
0.70	70%	7/10

hypothesis. We can say that it is unlikely that we would have found these results *if the null hypothesis were correct*. In short, a *statistically significant result* is a *rare result* – a result we would not expect to get if the null hypothesis were true.

To re-emphasise, the probability value (*p* value, for short), or significance value, is the result of most statistical tests. It is often what we are most interested in because it tells us whether our theory was supported (if *p* is less than 0.05) or not (if *p* is greater than 0.05).

DIRECTIONAL AND NON-DIRECTIONAL HYPOTHESES

> **Crucial concept** A *one-tailed hypothesis* (or directional hypothesis) says that there will be an effect and specifies the direction of the effect. A *two-tailed hypothesis* (or non-directional hypothesis) says that there will be an effect but that effect could go in either direction.

As we saw in Chapter I, hypotheses can be of two kinds. A hypothesis can specify that an effect will happen (i.e. that there will be a difference between two groups) without specifying the direction that difference will be in. This is known as a *non-directional* or *two-tailed* hypothesis. Alternatively, a hypothesis can specify both the effect and the direction of that effect. This is known as a *directional* or *one-tailed* hypothesis.

- Example of a one-tailed hypothesis: *Participants who are given alcohol will show* better *performance at a task than participants given a placebo.*

- Example of a two-tailed hypothesis: *Participants who are given alcohol will show* different *performance at a task than participants given a placebo.*

> **Crucial tip** It is usually better to use a non-directional hypothesis, because if your results are significant but in the opposite direction, the null hypothesis cannot be rejected. You are then left having to say that your results do not show anything when it is rather clear that they do show something (though not what you expected).

CONDITIONAL PROBABILITIES

To understand what we mean by the *probability value* associated with a statistical test we need to understand something called *conditional probabilities*.

A probability value associated with a statistical test tells us the probability of that result given that the null hypothesis was true. What we did not consider was the probability that the null hypothesis was true given that result.

This seems like a bit of a strange thing – it may sound as though I wrote the same thing twice, and then I said that the two things were different. So let's have a closer look.

Here is a concrete example:

There is a club frequented by students, called Henrietta's.[2] Monday night is student night, and alcoholic drinks are cheap. Therefore, most people who are in the club on a Monday night are drunk.

---

[2] Names have been changed to protect the innocent.

We can say that the chance or probability of a person in Henrietta's being drunk are quite high. We could say the same thing in another way: that the probability of someone being drunk, given that they are in Henrietta's, is high. If we wanted to write this more mathematically, we could use symbols to show where people were and what condition they were in. So:

> D means drunk.
> H means Henrietta's.
> | is a mathematical symbol which means 'given that'.
> p is short for probability.

If 80% of the people in Henrietta's are drunk, the chances are 0.8 that any one person in Henrietta's is drunk (because 0.8 is another way of writing 80%).

We could write:

$$p(D \mid H) = 0.8$$

which is a quick way of saying that the probability of someone being drunk, given that they are in Henrietta's, is quite high.

However, there are many other places where people get drunk on a Monday night – there are other clubs and pubs, and people get drunk at home. So just because someone is drunk, it doesn't mean that they are in Henrietta's. In fact, probably only 1%, or 1 in 100, of the people in the city who are drunk on a Monday night are in Henrietta's. So the probability that someone is in Henrietta's, given that they are drunk, is only 0.01.

Using the same symbols as we used before we can say that:

$$p(H \mid D) = 0.01$$

This means that the two probabilities are not the same – if you turn the conditions around, they are not equal. We can write this as:

$$p(H \mid D) \neq p(D \mid H)$$

($\neq$ is a symbol which means 'not equal to.')

So what has this got to do with us? When we have done a statistical test, we get a probability associated with our null hypothesis. It is tempting to think of this probability as a probability of H_0 being true, given the data that we have collected. We could write this as:

$$p(H \mid D)$$

It would be very nice if this were the case, because it would allow us to make very strong statements about our theory and our hypothesis. Unfortunately, we can't make statements like $p(H \mid D)$. What we can say is that we have a probability of having the data that we have collected, given that the null hypothesis is true. We can write this as:

$$p(D \mid H)$$

And just like before:

$$p(H \mid D) \neq p(D \mid H)$$

If we were able to talk about $p(H \mid D)$ we would be able to make strong statements about the null hypothesis. We would be talking about the probability of the null hypothesis being true. However, we are not talking directly about the probability of the null hypothesis. We are only talking about the probability of the data, which (as we have seen) is not the same thing, and does not allow us to make such a strong case.

Section summary

In this section we have introduced some of the ideas behind statistical significance. First, we considered probability, which is the likelihood of an event and ranges from 0 to 1.

Then we considered what is meant by statistical significance. Statistical significance is the probability of the result we have occurring if the null hypothesis (in the population) is true. A statistically significant result would be rare if the null hypothesis (in the population) were correct.

We also looked at two issues in statistical significance: we considered that a statistically significant result can regulate to a one-tailed (directional) hypothesis or a two-tailed (non-directional) hypothesis. A two-tailed hypothesis is usually preferable. We then looked at conditional probabilities, and we considered that a statistically significant result does not tell us about the probability of our null hypothesis being correct, as we might be tempted to believe. Rather, it tells us about the probability of the result *given that* the null hypothesis is correct. This is a difficult concept to understand, but means that we should be careful not to say that we have proved or disproved a hypothesis.

Section 2	When things go wrong

What are you studying?

In this section we will look at the errors that are made in significance testing. First we will explain the different types of error that can be made – to make life simpler we will use an analogy of going to the shop to fetch milk. We will then look at how likely you are to make different kinds of error and what affects the probability of making a different kind of error.

Statistical significance and errors

> Crucial concept   A *type I error* is a false rejection of the null hypothesis – a false positive.

> Crucial concept   A *type II error* is a false failure to reject the null hypothesis – a false negative.

Just because a result is statistically significant does not mean that it is *true*. In addition, just because a result is not statistically significant does not mean that it is *false*. It is possible that an error was made. There are costs associated with each of these types of error. Let's use an example to try to make it clearer. You want some milk, but only one shop is open and it may have run out of milk. You are trying to decide whether you should bother going to the shop to get some milk, but you don't know whether the shop will have any.

You have a theory that there will be milk in the shop. If you go to the shop and find that there is no milk there, then your theory was wrong. This is a little like saying that you have rejected your null hypothesis when the null hypothesis was actually correct.

If you decide that your theory is wrong so you don't go to the shop but there was milk there, then your theory was correct but you incorrectly thought it was incorrect. This is a little like saying that you have not rejected your null hypothesis, when the null hypothesis was false and should have been rejected.

How sure do you have to be that there will be milk in the shop before you go? The value that determines how sure you have to be is alpha. In psychology, we use the value 0.05 as the value for alpha, the cut-off, before we say that the null hypothesis is rejected. We will not say that we have a result, unless the probability that we are wrong is less than 0.05 (i.e. 5% or 1 in 20). This means that you will not go to the shop unless you are fairly sure that there is milk there – you will not go unless you are 95% sure that you are going to find milk when you get there.

Although this seems like quite a stringent level of alpha – we are having to be very sure before we go to the shop – this makes sense in psychology (and science in general). If you only go to the shop when there is a 0.05 (or less) probability that there is not going to be milk there, you will get milk 95% of the time.

If psychologists stood up and claimed to have made discoveries but these so-called discoveries were not soundly based, psychology textbooks would be full of meaningless results. In the same way as you could go the shop and regularly return with no milk, psychologists would look for some phenomena and regularly find it when there was no such thing occurring.

The outcome of a significance testing, and the outcome of your decision to go to the shop or not, are binary decisions. (That is a clever way of saying that you can say *yes*, I believe that there is milk, or *no*, I believe that there is no milk.) The state of the shop is also one of two things: there is milk, or there is no milk.[3] Thus there are four possible combinations of events, as shown in Table 7.2.

Decision made	State of the shop	Result
Went to shop	Milk	Correct acceptance
Stayed home	No milk	Correct reject
Went to shop	No milk	Type I error
Stayed home	Milk	Type II error

Table 7.2: Combination of events.

In the first scenario, we have gone to the shop and there was milk there. This was OK.

In the second scenario, we stayed at home and there was no milk in the shop. This was OK too.

In the third scenario, we went to the shop but there was no milk when we got there. This was a *type I error*.

In the final scenario, we stayed at home, thinking there was no milk in the shop, when there was milk. This was also an error. We could have gone to the shop and got milk, and as a result have had to drink our coffee black, go without cornflakes and generally have a bad time. This is called a *type II error*.

Crucial tip

To remember which is a type I error and which is a type II error, use the following memory aid:

If you made a type I error, (thinking there was milk, but there wasn't), you were optimistic. If you made a type II error (thinking there was no milk, when there was) you were pessimistic.

Optimistic: type I error.
Pessimistic: type II error.

The order of errors is the same order as O and P in the alphabet.

---

[3] This may not be the case. There may only be skimmed milk when you wanted semi-skimmed. But we will pretend we don't know that now.

Error rates

We can find out how likely it is that we have made a type I error or a type II error. It is very easy to determine the probability that you have made a type I error, but very difficult to determine if you have made a type II error. (Remember that a type I error is an optimistic error, or a false positive, and a type II error is a pessimistic error, or a false negative.)

TYPE I ERRORS

The probability of making a type I error (that is rejecting your null hypothesis when the correct result would have been to accept it – the equivalent of going to the shop and finding it empty) is equal to the value for alpha. If alpha is 0.05, then there is a probability of 0.05 (or 5%, or 1 in 20) you will have made a type I error, and falsely accepted the hypothesis.

TYPE II ERRORS

If your hypothesis is false, you can do one of two things: you can reject it and be correct, or you can fail to reject it and make a type II error. The probability of correctly rejecting your null hypothesis is called *power*. The probability of falsely failing to reject your null hypothesis, i.e. making a type II error, is called beta (β). Because one of those two things must happen, we know that:

$$power + beta = 1$$

and therefore it follows that:

$$beta = 1 - power$$

So to calculate the type II error rate, we need to first calculate the power and then subtract the value we get for the power from 1.

Testing a hypothesis can be thought of as like looking for something; your probability of finding what you are looking for depends upon how hard you look and what you are looking for – the bigger the object, the easier it will be to find.

So to increase power, you need to look harder for evidence to reject the null hypothesis. There are two ways of looking harder for this evidence:

- The first way is to use a higher value for alpha. You pay the price of an increase in the type I error rate and get the reward of more power, and therefore a lower type II error rate.[4]
- The second way is to use a larger sample. By decreasing the uncertainty about what we have, we increase our ability to say we have found something. If we look through more things, we have a greater chance of finding something.

The probability of your finding something also depends upon how large it is. In psychological research, this means the size of the effect we are looking for – how much effect does our independent variable have? For example, the number of hours you spend studying for an exam has a large effect on how well you do in the exam, and therefore this effect should be easy to find. If the colour of the walls in the exam room has any effect on how well you do in the exam, this

---

[4] It has been noted that, as the night wears on, the girls (and the boys) get better looking. This can be explained in terms of alpha being raised, to increase power. The criterion is lowered to increase the probability of finding a suitable partner before the night is over.

effect will be very small, and therefore very difficult to find. The problem is that, in psychology, we don't know what we are looking for before we have found it, and so we don't know how big it is going to be.

If we know the size of the thing we are looking for, the size of the sample we will use and the value for alpha, the power can be calculated. (Table 7.3 summarises the effects of different factors on power.) Power is calculated by looking in a table in a book, for example Cohen (1988) or Kraemer and Thiemann (1987), or by using a specialised computer program.

Factor	What happens to power as it increases?	What happens to type II error rate as it increases?
Sample size	Increases	Decreases
Effect size	Increases	Decreases
Alpha	Increases	Decreases

Table 7.3: Summary of the effects of different factors on power.

Section summary

In this section we have considered type I errors and type II errors. A type I error is a false positive – it is an optimistic error and occurs when we think that we can reject our null hypothesis but we are wrong.

A type II error is a false negative – it is a pessimistic error and occurs when we think that we cannot reject our null hypothesis but we are wrong.

The probability of making a type I error is dependent upon the level of alpha that is used (usually 0.05). The probability of making a type II error is very difficult to work out, but is dependent on sample size, the size of the effect in the population and the value of alpha that is chosen.

Further reading

We have only had a very brief look at inferential statistics in this chapter. The area is more complex and more controversial than you might have imagined. A good start if you would like to explore the issues further is *Statistics as Principled Argument* by Robert Abelson (published by Erlbaum). Also, several chapters in the book *A Handbook for Data Analysis in the Behavioural Sciences: Methodological Issues*, edited by Keren and Lewis, examine the basis of inferential statistics in much more depth (also published by Erlbaum). A brief look at the logic of significance testing can be found in the book *Understanding Significance Testing*, by Mohr (published by Sage). If you are feeling stronger, two books could be recommended: the first, *Statistical Significance* by Chow (published by Sage), is a strong defence of significance tests against recent attacks, but you should be warned that the book is somewhat heavy going. The second book is *What If There Were No Significance Tests*, edited by Harlow, Mulaik and Steiger (published by Erlbaum). This lists arguments from both sides of the debate about the usefulness of statistical significance.

CHAPTER 8

USING
INFERENTIAL STATISTICS

Chapter summary

Studying this Chapter will help you to:

- Determine the most appropriate statistical test to use for a research question.
- Describe the circumstances where a non-parametric test should be used.
- Be able to report the results of common statistical tests.

Why do you need to know this?

When you carry out a research project, you analyse a sample of individuals. However, you are not just interested in that small group of individuals. You are interested in the *population* from which that sample is taken – you want to be able to *generalise* from your sample to the population. You take a hypothesis, for example:

> Students who work harder at statistics have fuller, happier lives than students who do not work so hard at statistics.

and its corresponding null hypothesis:

> Students who work harder at statistics do not have fuller, happier lives than students who do not work so hard at statistics.

You might find that, in your sample, this hypothesis is supported – the students in your sample who worked harder at statistics did indeed have fuller, happier lives. However, we are not just interested in the students in your sample. If we were only interested in the characteristics of your sample, the findings of your study (and every other study in psychology) would have very limited applicability. What we want to be able to do is to *infer* something from your *sample* to the *population*. If we want to infer something, as we saw in the previous chapter, we are going to have to use inferential statistics. This chapter is about the statistical procedures that are used when we want to generalise from a sample to a population.

Crucial concepts

These are the key terms you will meet in this chapter:

Chi-square test	Parameter
Confidence interval	Parametric
Correlation	Pearson correlation
Friedman's test	Repeated measures ANOVA
Independent groups t-test	Repeated measures t-test
Interaction effect	Sign test
Kruskal-Wallis test	Spearman correlation
Levels (of an independent variable)	Standard error
Mann-Whitney U Test	Statistic
McNemar's test	Wilcoxon rank sum test
Non-parametric	Wilcoxon signed-ranks test
One-way ANOVA	

In this chapter, we are going to look at inferential statistics – what are normally called statistical tests. We are not going to look at how to *do* the calculations, because they are not very interesting, and they are not very hard. Yes, that's correct – they are not very hard. If you have a computer program (and most students nowadays do have access to a computer program) they are easy. If you don't have a computer program, they are still easy (they are slightly more time-consuming, but they are still easy) – they involve doing arithmetic, which might be tortuous and dull, but isn't hard. Instead of focusing on the easy stuff, we are going to focus on the parts that students get wrong much more often – knowing what a particular test does, knowing when to use it, and knowing how to write about it.

We are going to look at some simple statistical tests. We will look at the standard error, which is used for one variable; then we will look at statistical tests for analysing experimental and quasi-experimental data. Finally, we will look at correlations.

Section I	Introduction

In this section we introduce ideas about why we need to use inferential statistical tests to test hypotheses. We introduce a very important distinction – that between parametric statistical tests and non-parametric statistical tests.

Two types of test

> Crucial concept   *Parametric tests* are more powerful tests which make certain assumptions (normal distribution, interval level measurement) of your data.

> Crucial concept   *Non-parametric tests* are less powerful tests which make fewer assumptions of your data.

Statistical tests can be broadly divided into two types: parametric tests and non-parametric tests. (Some statisticians argue that non-parametric is a poor name, and prefer to call them 'distribution-free' tests.) If you can do a parametric test it is usually better to do so, but they cannot be used in all circumstances. Parametric tests make assumptions about the data that must be satisfied for the tests to work properly. If the assumptions are not satisfied, the results of the test may be misleading.

All parametric tests assume that:

1. the data are measured on an interval or ratio scale (see Chapter 4);
2. the data are normally distributed (exactly what needs to be normally distributed varies, and we shall discuss this later).

Non-parametric tests are used with ordinal data, and do not make assumptions about the shape of the distribution.

> Crucial tip   The assumptions that have to be made when we use parametric tests are the same as those we have to make when using the mean and standard deviation. If the mean is an appropriate measure of central tendency, you should probably be using a parametric test. If you are using the median, you probably should be using a non-parametric test.

It should be noted that most of the parametric tests that we will consider are *robust* against violations of assumptions. To say that a test is robust means that the tests will still give useful answers even when the assumptions behind them are violated, as long as the violations are not too serious.

Section summary

In this section we have looked at what we are going to cover in the rest of the chapter, and introduced parametric statistical tests and non-parametric statistical tests.

Section 2	Confidence intervals – making single variable inferences

What are you studying?

In this section we will look at confidence limits and confidence intervals. We will look at how confidence limits are used, and then see how varying the sample size and varying the degree of confidence we want to have in our statements affect the confidence limits.

The first type of inferential statistic that we shall look at is the *confidence interval*. The *standard error* is used for making inferences from a *sample statistic* about a particular value of a *parameter* in the population.

> Crucial concept   A *parameter* and a *statistic* refer to anything that can be measured and given a value. A parameter is the value in the population. A statistic is the value that we have found in our sample. If we are interested in the mean height of psychology students in the UK, the true mean height is a *parameter* – sometimes called a *population parameter*. If we measure the height of a sample of psychology students and find the average, we will have a *statistic* – sometimes called a sample statistic. We estimate a population parameter using a sample statistic.

When we have calculated our sample statistic, we have a *sample estimate of a population parameter*. The sample statistic is our best guess at the value of the population parameter. To help us to estimate the population parameter, we can calculate (or ask a computer to calculate for us) a *confidence interval* around the parameter estimate – this tells us within what range of numbers the true value is likely to be.

> Crucial concept   The *standard error* of a parameter estimate is the standard error of the sampling distribution of that statistic. The standard error is not very interesting on its own but it is used to calculate the confidence intervals.

> Crucial concept   If we calculate the 95% *confidence intervals* of a mean, that indicates that 95% of the time the mean of another sample will lie within those intervals.

This will make more sense when we look at an example. Suppose we are interested in knowing the mean number of textbooks on research methods and statistics owned by psychology students. We want to know the population parameter value. To find out the population value for sure, we would need to ask every student how many books they owned – this is unfeasible, as we do not have the time or the inclination to do it. Instead, we take a representative sample (see Chapter 5 to see what we mean by a representative sample) of students, and find out how many textbooks the students in our sample own.

Suppose we ask 10 students how many books they own, and we find that the mean number of books owned is 12 and the standard deviation is 4. Our *sample statistic* of the population value is

12, but we want to know what the population value is likely to be. We would be very lucky indeed to find that our sample statistic matched the population parameter.

We calculate something called the 95% *confidence limit*, and in this case, with our sample of 10 students, it is equal to 3.48. This result means that we can say, with a probability of 0.95 (i.e. be 95% sure), that the true value of the population mean is likely to be between 12 − 3.48 = 8.52, and 12 + 3.48 = 15.48. If we were to say that the true mean value number of textbooks owned by psychology students is between 8.52 and 15.48, we will only be wrong 5% of the time (i.e. 1 time in 20) and we will be correct 95% of the time (i.e. 19 times in 20).

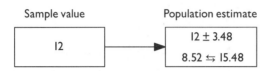

Being wrong 1 time in 20 is reasonably accurate, but may not be accurate enough for our needs. Being right 19 times out of 20 is not enough if the consequences of being wrong are very serious. If we want a higher degree of accuracy, we can use different limits to calculate our confidence intervals. The 99% confidence limit, for example, is 4.85. If we want to be 99% sure that we have included the population parameter within our limits, we need to say that the true value of the mean is from 7.15 to 16.85.

In this first example, we only collected data from 10 students. We could improve the accuracy of our predictions by collecting from a larger number. If we asked 20 students, and we found we got the same mean and standard deviation (although this is unlikely), the confidence limit would shrink to 2.18 and therefore we could be 95% sure that the population parameter value was between 9.82 and 14.18.

There are two things to note here. The first is that, if you want to have more confidence that you have included the population value in your confidence interval, you are going to have larger confidence intervals. The second is that if you have a larger sample size, your confidence intervals will shrink. When you have small sample sizes, a small increase in sample size causes a large reduction in confidence limits. With larger sample sizes, a large increase in sample size causes a smaller reduction in the confidence limits.

Confidence intervals are often plotted on graphs – a point representing the sample statistic and a line extending to show the range of the intervals, as in Figure 8.1.

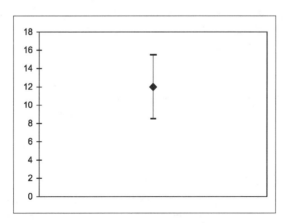

Figure 8.1: Chart showing a mean value of 12 and upper and lower 95% confidence intervals.

To calculate the standard error of a mean, you have to make the two assumptions made by parametric tests: that you have a *normal distribution* and *interval data*.

In this section, we used the mean to illustrate confidence limits and intervals, but confidence limits and intervals can be calculated for many different kinds of sample statistics. Most common is the mean, but you will also see (and can calculate) confidence intervals for correlations and regression lines. It is not possible to calculate a confidence interval for all sample statistics – most notably there is no formula to calculate confidence intervals for the median.

Section summary

The confidence limits of a sample statistic (or parameter estimate) are used to give us some idea of the value of that parameter in the population. The size of confidence limits are affected by the sample size: larger sample sizes lead to smaller confidence limits. If we want to have more confidence that we have captured the population value within our confidence limit, the confidence limits will be wider.

Section 3	Analysing data from experiments – interval/ordinal dependent variable

What are you studying?

This section will look at statistical tests for analysing data from experiments and quasi-experiments. First, we remind ourselves about the structure of experiments, and then have a look at the process of selecting a statistical test. We begin with experiments with one independent variable, first looking at between-participants designs and then within-participants designs. Within each of these designs we first look at the simple case of a study with two levels of one independent variable, and then more than two levels. We then consider the case of experiments with more than one independent variable – here we need to think about interactions. Finally, we look at the possibility of more complex designs.

Choosing a statistical test

To decide which statistical test you should use, you need to know three things:

1. whether it is appropriate to use a parametric test or not;
2. whether the independent variable is within-participants (repeated measures) or between-participants (independent groups);
3. how many *levels* the independent variable has.

The structure of experiments

In Chapter 2, we looked at the structure of experiments in some detail. In this section, we will look at how to analyse data from experimental research. If you are not familiar with the material in Chapter 2, you can have a look at the 'Quick Reminder' below, or it might be worth quickly revising Chapter 2 before reading this chapter.

Quick reminder

An experiment investigated the effects of three types of noise (silence, hammering, music) on the ability to learn two types of word (abstract and concrete). We would describe this experiment as having:

- two independent variables:

  - *noise*, which has three levels: silence, hammering, music;
  - *word type*, which has two levels: abstract and concrete;

- one dependent variable:

  - *number of words remembered.*

The independent variables could each be between-participants or within-participants. If the independent variables were between participants, different people would take part in each level. If the independent variables were within-participants, the same people would take part in all levels.

An experiment comprises one or more independent variables each of which has two or more levels, and one or more dependent variables.

In this section we will look at:

- experiments with one independent variable;
- experiments with more than one independent variable.

We will first consider the case of experiments with interval or ordinal dependent variables, and then move on to experiments with nominal dependent variables.

Figure 8.2 shows a flow diagram that will help you to choose an appropriate statistical test when you are analysing data from an experiment that has one dependent variable. Table 8.1 shows the same information represented in a different way – you can use whichever you feel most comfortable with. We will examine each of the tests in turn.

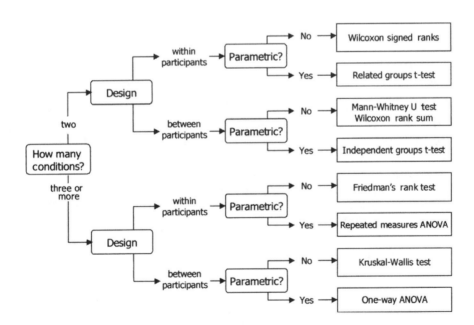

Figure 8.2: Decision chart for analysing experimental data
with ordinal/interval dependent variable.

| | Between-participants design | | Within-participants design | |
	Parametric	Non-parametric	Parametric	Non-parametric
Two levels	Independent groups t-test	Mann-Whitney U test Wilcoxon rank sum test	Repeated measures t-test	Wilcoxon signed ranks test
Three or more levels	One-way ANOVA	Kruskal-Wallis test	One-way repeated measures ANOVA	Friedman's rank test

Table 8.1: Decision table for analysing experimental data
with ordinal/interval dependent variable.

Experiments with one independent variable

BETWEEN-PARTICIPANTS DESIGN

Two levels of independent variable

In the simplest form of experiment, we have one independent variable that has two levels. For example, we might be investigating the effects of noise on learning. To do this we would randomly divide our participants into two groups. We might give each group the task of learning a list of 100 words in five minutes. Then, we would ask them to recall as many of the words as possible. One group (the control group) would undertake this task in silence. The second group of people would undertake the learning task while a tape player was playing classical music in the room.

We first need to decide whether to use a parametric or a non-parametric test. As we saw in the previous section, a parametric test is preferable if the assumptions that it makes are satisfied. All parametric tests make the following assumptions:

1. *Normal distribution.* We must check first that the data are normally distributed (see Chapter 7). To determine if the data are normally distributed you can draw a histogram or calculate skewness and kurtosis statistics. Note that it is the distribution *within* each group that must be normal; we do not require that the distribution for both groups combined is normal.

2. *Interval data.* To use a parametric test, we also need to consider whether our dependent variable is measured on an interval scale (see Chapter 5). In the case of our experiment, the dependent variable − number of words recalled − is measured on an interval scale.

If we follow the decision chart shown in Figure 8.2, you will see that, if we have satisfied the above two assumptions, we are able to do an independent groups t-test. If we have not satisfied the assumptions, we should do a Mann-Whitney U test or a Wilcoxon rank sum test.

We will examine both of these options in turn.

The independent groups t-test

This test also has other names, for example the unpaired t-test, the between-subjects t-test or the uncorrelated t-test.

> Crucial concept   The *independent groups t-test* compares the mean of two unrelated sam-
> ples to determine whether the two unrelated samples are significantly
> different from one another.

We have already assumed that we are dealing with interval data and a normal distribution – these are the assumptions made by all parametric tests. The independent groups *t*-test makes an additional assumption – called *homogeneity of variance*. For the data to satisfy the assumption of *homogeneity of variance*, the variances (standard deviations) of the two samples should be the same, or at least similar. However, the *t*-test is robust against violation of this assumption – the standard deviations can be fairly different and the *t*-test will still perform satisfactorily as long as the sample sizes of the two groups are similar. A general rule of thumb to apply is that as long as one of the standard deviations is not more than twice the other, you should be OK.

Crucial tip	It is often important to note whether a letter which represents something is in upper case or lower case. Sometimes an upper case letter means something different to a lower case letter (*r* and *R* are not the same thing).

It is also possible to correct the *t*-test so that this assumption of homogeneity of variance is not necessary. This correction for non-homogeneity of variance is difficult to calculate by hand, but if you analyse your data on a computer, you will probably find that the correction is done automatically.

You will sometimes find that the value for *t* is negative – this doesn't matter, and you can ignore the minus sign.

When you report an independent groups *t*-test, you should report the value of *t*, the *degrees of freedom* (*df*) and the *probability value*, for example: $t = 3.4$, $df = 24$, $p = 0.002$ (2-tailed).

Student's *t*-test

In some textbooks you might see the *t*-test referred to as 'Student's *t*-test'. When I first encountered the Student's *t*-test, I imagined that it must be some sort of downgraded, easier *t*-test for students, and there must be a lecturer's *t*-test which would be a proper *t*-test. You might not be surprised to hear that I was wrong, that is not why the Student's *t*-test is so called, but there is an interesting story behind the name.

William Gosset, a graduate of mathematics and chemistry from Oxford University, went to work for the Guinness brewery in Dublin. He was given the task of comparing two batches of ingredients to decide whether they were of the same quality or not. To do this, he developed the *t*-test to compare two independent samples. When he published his research, he did it under the pseudonym of 'A. Student'. There are two different reasons given for why he published his work under a pseudonym. The first is that he was not allowed to publish the research under his own name because the Guinness brewery was concerned about letting its rivals know about their techniques. The second is that Gosset was a rather shy and modest man who did not seek accolades for himself. He called himself 'A. Student' as a tribute to Karl Pearson, who had been his teacher.

Mann-Whitney U test / Wilcoxon rank sum test

Crucial concept	The *Mann-Whitney U-test* and the *Wilcoxon rank sum test* are non-parametric tests for independent designs.

The Mann-Whitney U test and the Wilcoxon rank-sum test are used when the parametric assumptions for an independent groups *t*-test are not satisfied (i.e. the data are not normally distributed or not measured on an interval scale). These tests are the non-parametric correspondents of the independent groups t-test. The two tests are equivalent – they will both give identical answers and it doesn't matter which one you use.

The Mann-Whitney U test is slightly simpler to calculate than the Wilcoxon rank sum test, and so if you are doing your analysis by hand you should use the former. (There is a second Wilcoxon test which we will come across later on, so if you use the Mann-Whitney U test, you will be at less risk of confusing the two.)

To report a Mann-Whitney U test, you should give the value of U (the test statistic), the size of both of the groups and the probability value, for example: $U = 22.5$, $N_1 = 6$, $N_2 = 8$, $p = 0.85$.

A Wilcoxon rank sum test is reported in the same way: $W = 43.5$, $N_1 = 6$, $N_2 = 8$, $p = 0.85$.

If you have a large sample, you might have to convert the U or W statistic to a Z statistic. In this case, you should also report the Z statistic.

Three or more levels of independent variable

In a slightly more complex experiment, we might test participants under three levels of an independent variable. In a previous example when we were investigating the effects of noise on learning, we had two groups, *silence* and *noise*. However, we might be interested in investigating the effects of different *kinds* of noise. If this were the case, we could then have three groups.

- silence;

- classical music;

- hammering.

These three groups constitute the three levels of independent variable.

One-way analysis of variance

Crucial concept   *One-way analysis of variance* is a parametric test which compares the means of three or more groups.

Analysis of variance (usually shortened to ANOVA) is a whole family of statistical tests. A one-way analysis of variance compares the means of three or more groups to see if the means of the three groups are different from one another.

ANOVA tests are parametric statistical tests, which means that it makes the same assumptions as those made by the t-test:

- normal distribution;

- interval data.

A one-way ANOVA, like the *t*-test, makes an assumption *of homogeneity of variance* and it assumes that the standard deviations in the different conditions are equal or at least similar to each other. In the case of the *t*-test we saw that it is possible to carry out a correction for violation of homogeneity of variance, but such a correction is not usually possible for ANOVA. In addition, in the same way as a *t*-test, many computer programs will calculate Levene's test for homogeneity of variance which will test this assumption. However, a one-way ANOVA is robust against violation of this assumption.

When you report the results of an ANOVA, you should report the test statistic, *F*, *two* sets of degrees of freedom (not just one as with the *t*-test) and the probability value, for example: $F = 6.62$, *df* = 2, 15, $p = 0.009$.

Finally, you should note that one-way ANOVA tests the null hypothesis that:

Mean of group 1 = Mean of group 2 = Mean of group 3 . . . etc.

Because the null hypothesis states that the means are all equal, the null hypothesis can be false for more than one reason. It may be, for example, that group 1 and group 2 are significantly different from one another; it may be that group 2 is significantly different from group 3; and so on. Because a significant value for F can have more than one possible meaning, you may have to investigate your data further to find out what differences exist.

The first and simplest approach to checking the differences is to plot the means, along with their 95% confidence intervals, on a graph. This graph will often demonstrate where the differences lie. For example, Figure 8.3 shows the mean and 95% confidence intervals for the number of words remembered by the three groups who learned in *silence*, *classical music* and *hammering* conditions. It can be seen that there is little difference between the silence and classical music group, but the overall score for the hammering group is much lower – there is also no overlap between the 95% confidence interval for the hammering group and the other two groups.

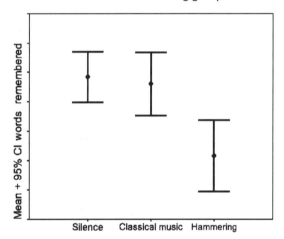

Figure 8.3: Graph showing means and 95% confidence intervals
of memory scores under three noise conditions.

Another way to make comparisons between groups is to carry out *post hoc* tests. There are two types of *post hoc* tests – *planned contrasts* and *unplanned contrasts*. Use *planned contrasts* when you have a theoretical reason to believe that some specific differences will occur and you want to investigate those differences. Use *unplanned contrasts* to compare every group with every other group.

Kruskal-Wallis Test

The Kruskal-Wallis test is the non-parametric equivalent of a one-way ANOVA for comparing the distributions of three or more groups when the assumptions for using one-way ANOVA have been violated. The rank test gives χ^2 (written as chi-square if you don't have the symbol available, and pronounced 'ky' – like 'sky' but without the 's'). The χ^2, along with its degrees of freedom and associated probability, should be reported, for example: $\chi^2 = 9.1$, $df = 2$, $p = 0.011$.

WITHIN-PARTICIPANTS DESIGN

A within-participants design means that the same individuals are tested and measured under all conditions of the independent variable. While this design is more efficient in that fewer participants are required, it does, however, raise some complex methodological issues which are discussed in Chapter 2.

Two levels of independent variable

As with the *independent groups design*, the first thing that you must decide is whether to use a parametric or a non-parametric test. To remind you, the parametric test assumes that the data are:

- normally distributed;
- interval level data.

Repeated measures t-test

> **Crucial concept** The *repeated measure t-test* is a parametric test used to compare the means of two related groups (usually the same people measured twice).

The repeated measures *t*-test is very similar to the independent groups *t*-test that we looked at in the previous section. You will sometimes see the repeated measures *t*-test referred to as the matched pairs *t*-test, the correlated *t*-test or the within-participants *t*-test. All of these are the same thing.

To carry out a *repeated measures t*-test, each participant has to have been measured twice, so you should have pairs of values for each individual.

The repeated measures *t*-test assumes that the data are normally distributed, just like the independent groups *t*-test, but the assumption is a little bit different. This time, we do not assume that the raw scores are normally distributed; rather we assume that the *differences* between the scores are normally distributed. If we were carrying out an experiment on the effects of noise on learning, we would test each person under two conditions, once in silence and once in a noisy environment.

We would then have two scores for each person, as shown in Table 8.2 – one from the *noise* condition, and one from the *silence* condition. The difference between these scores is shown in the 'difference' column in Table 8.2. It is these *difference scores* that we assume to have a normal distribution, although as with the independent groups *t*-test the test is quite robust to violations of this assumption. The repeated measures *t*-test does not make any assumption about homogeneity of variance.

Silence	Noise	Difference
50	35	15
40	45	−5
38	22	16
91	86	5

Table 8.2: Scores from repeated measures experiment on learning and noise.

When you have carried out a repeated measures t-test, you will sometimes find that the value for t is negative, and, as with the independent groups t-test, you can ignore the minus sign. When you report a repeated measures t-test, you should report the value for t, the degrees of freedom and the probability, for example: $t = 0.38$, $df = 5$, $p = 0.723$.

The Wilcoxon signed ranks Test

> Crucial concept The *Wilcoxon signed ranks test* is a non-parametric test to compare two related groups (usually the same people measured twice).

The Wilcoxon signed ranks test is used when the assumptions of the repeated measures t-test are violated. The test statistic from a Wilcoxon test is T, although sometimes this will be converted to a Z. To report a Wilcoxon signed ranks test, you should report the T or Z statistic, along with the N and the probability, for example: $T = 8.0$, $N = 6$, $p = 0.60$, or $Z = 5.26$, $N = 6$, $p = 0.60$.

Three or more levels of an independent variable

You have seen that the *independent groups* design can have three or more levels of the independent variable. A *repeated measures* study can also be designed with three or more levels of the *independent* variable. In the previous example we tested participants under two different conditions, silence and noise. As before, we might be interested in investigating the effects of different *kinds* of noise, and if this were the case we might have three groups:

- silence;
- classical music;
- hammering.

Repeated measures analysis of variance

> Crucial concept *Repeated measures ANOVA* is a parametric test used to compare three (or more) related groups (usually the same people measured on each occasion).

Repeated measures analysis of variance is the second member of the ANOVA family that we have encountered. Repeated measures ANOVA makes the assumptions that we encountered before:

- normal distribution;
- interval data.

A repeated measures ANOVA also makes a nasty third assumption called *sphericity*, or *homogeneity of covariance*. This assumption means that the *variances* of the different variables must be equal, and that the *correlations* between the variables must also be equal. Repeated measures ANOVA is not especially robust against violation of this assumption so we do need to worry about it. Luckily, we only need to worry about it a little, because when you carry out a repeated measures ANOVA using a computer, it should automatically test the sphericity assumption for you, and automatically carry out a correction which compensates for violation of the assumption. There is more than one type of correction, but the most commonly used is called the *Greenhouse-Geisser epsilon* correction.

When you report a repeated measures ANOVA, you should report the F, df and p values, as with the one-way ANOVA.

Friedman's test

> **Crucial concept** *Friedman's test* is a non-parametric test used to compare three (or more) related groups (usually the same people measured on each occasion).

Friedman's test is used when the assumptions for a repeated measures analysis of variance have been violated. The test statistic is a χ^2, which should be reported with its associated df and probability value, for example: $\chi^2 = 17.3$, $df = 5$, $p = 0.0039$.

Interactions: more than one independent variable

> **Crucial concept** An *interaction effect* occurs when the effect of one variable is dependent upon the level of a second independent variable.

Experiments are not limited to one independent variable. If an experiment has two independent variables, we are interested in the effect of each of those independent variables. However, we are also interested in a third effect – the *interaction effect*.

An interaction effect occurs when two variables do not simply add together their influence; rather they combine in some more complex way. Consider the following example:

An experiment was carried out to investigate the effects of using the 'method of loci' in learning a list of words. (The method of loci is a method of improving memory, which involves visualising the words to be remembered in specific locations.) Participants were split into two groups. One group was trained in the use of the method of loci, the second group were given no such training. The first independent variable is the *method of loci*.

The participants were then further split. One half of each group was asked to learn a list of concrete words – i.e. easily visualised objects such as 'chair', 'potato', 'bottle'. The second half of each group was asked to remember a list of abstract words – words that are not easily visualised, and refer to abstract concepts, such as 'love', 'justice', and 'reality'.

The results of the experiment are shown in Table 8.3. Looking first at the mean scores in the end column, you can see that the mean score for the *method of loci* group (23) is considerably higher than the mean score for the *control* group (12). We would therefore conclude that the method of loci improves people's ability to remember words. Second, if we look at the mean scores for the concrete and abstract words, we can see that the mean score for the *concrete* words (22) is higher than the mean score for the *abstract* words (13). We can therefore conclude that concrete words are easier to remember than abstract words. The two effects of the independent variables are referred to as *main effects*.

		Word type		Mean
		Concrete	Abstract	
Used method of loci?	No	14	10	12
	Yes	30	16	23
	Mean	22	13	17.5

Table 8.3: Results of experiment examining the effectiveness of the method of loci in remembering concrete and abstract words.

If we stop there, we have failed to tell the whole story – there is a third question to ask of the data. Is the effect of using the method of loci the same, regardless of whether we have concrete or abstract words? The easiest way to answer this third question is to plot a chart, such as Figure 8.4. This chart shows that the effect of the method of loci is to improve both abstract and concrete words, but the improvement in the concrete words is much greater than the improvement in the abstract words. This difference in improvement because of the method of loci effect is called an *interaction effect*.

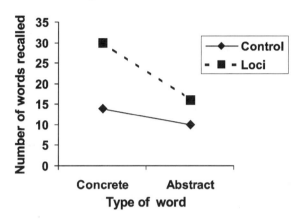

Figure 8.4: Results of method of loci study in chart format. The effect of the method of loci is to improve both abstract and concrete words, but the effect is greater for the abstract words than the concrete words.

Crucial tip   **Different slopes for different folks**

A different way of thinking about an interaction effect is to think of a main effect as being a *slope*. The improvement in number of words recalled from concrete to abstract can be represented as a slope. If the improvement is different, according to whether the individuals used the method of loci or not, the slopes will differ. Gary McClelland refers to this as being 'different slopes for different folks'.

In an experiment that has two IVs, we are looking at three different effects and testing three different null hypotheses. In an experiment where the two IVs are the method of loci (present or absent) and the word type (abstract or concrete) we test three null hypotheses:

- There will be no difference between the number of abstract and concrete words recalled. This is a *main effect*.
- There will be no difference between the number of words recalled by the method of loci group and the control group. This is a *main effect*.
- The difference between the concrete words and the abstract words will not depend upon the use of the method of loci. This is an *interaction effect*.

In your practical reports, you need to make it clear which of these effects you are interested in testing and which effects are relevant for your theory. You also need to report the *F*, *df* and *p* for each of those tests.

Some more graphs showing different sorts of interactions are shown in Figures 8.5 to 8.8. In each graph there are two IVs. IV_1 is represented on the X axis, and consists of two groups, X and Y. IV_2 is represented by the two lines. A is represented by the solid line, B by the dashed line.

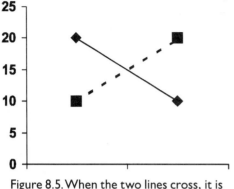

Figure 8.5. When the two lines cross, it is called a cross-over interaction. In this case, neither of the main effects is significant, but there is an interaction effect.

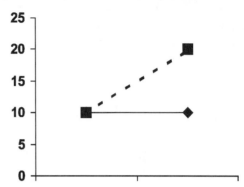

Figure 8.6: Both of the independent variables are having an effect on the dependent variable, but when we examine the plot, we can see that the effect of IV_1 depends very much on IV_2. There are two main effects and an interaction effect.

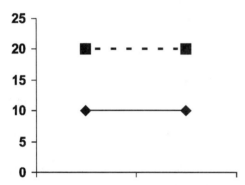

Figure 8.7: There is no interaction effect (the slopes are the same) and no effect of IV_1 – there is no difference between X and Y. There is a difference between Group A and Group B – this is a main effect.

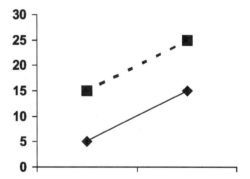

Figure 8.8: Both main effects are present, but there is no interaction effect – the slopes are the same.

More complex designs

If an experiment has two independent variables (such as we have been describing), and each of the independent variables has two levels, it is described as a 2 × 2 design.

It is possible to extend this design in two ways. First, the independent variable can have three levels. If the study had one IV with two levels, and one independent variable with three levels, it is described as a 3 × 2 design. A study which had one IV with four levels, and a second independent variable with three levels is described as a 4 × 3 design.

It is also possible for a study to have more than two independent variables. A study that has three independent variables, each of which has two levels, is called a 2 × 2 × 2 design. If a study has three independent variables (we will call them A, B and C), seven hypotheses are tested:

- the main effect of A;
- the main effect of B;
- the main effect of C;
- the A × B interaction effect (this is described as a *two-way interaction*);
- the A × C interaction effect;
- the B × C interaction effect;
- the A × B × C interaction effect (this is described as a *three-way interaction*).

In the examples that we have been discussing so far, we have only been talking about independent groups (between-participants) designs. It is also possible to have a repeated measures design with more than one independent variable. If we were to carry out an experiment to investigate the efficacy of the method of loci for remembering concrete and abstract words, each person would participate in all four conditions of the independent variable:

- method of loci, concrete words;
- method of loci, abstract words;
- no method of loci, concrete words;
- no method of loci, abstract words.

This would be called a 2 × 2 repeated measures design.

Finally, we can have an experiment in which one, or more, independent variables use independent groups, and one, or more, independent variables use repeated measures. These are referred to as a *mixed design*. If we were investigating the efficacy of the method of loci for abstract and concrete words with a mixed design, we would split participants into two groups: one group would use the method of loci, one would not, and both groups would be asked to remember both abstract and concrete words. To give the full title, we would refer to this as a 2 × 2 mixed design.

Section summary

In this section we have examined the use of eight tests for the analysis of data from experiments with one independent variable. We considered the decisions that are to be made, when deciding what test to use: whether the data can be considered to be interval, ordinal or nominal; whether the parametric assumptions (typically normality, but may be others) are satisfied; whether the independent variable has two or more levels. Additionally, we considered some more complex experimental designs, where there may be more than one independent variable, and the researcher would look for interactions between the independent variables.

Section 4	Experiments with a nominal dependent variable

What are you studying?

In this section we repeat the previous section, but this time we focus on experiments with nominal dependent variables. You will notice that this section is much shorter than the previous section – there are fewer tests for nominal data, and you need to be careful that you do not design an experiment with a nominal dependent variable that is difficult, or impossible, to analyse.

Nominal data are the simplest type of data – they count the number of individuals in the different categories. Analysis of simple experiments that have a nominal dependent variable is straightforward; surprisingly, in complex experiments this analysis becomes much more difficult.

One independent variable

INDEPENDENT GROUPS

If you have carried out an experiment that used an independent groups design, your data will consist of a *contingency table*.

For example, you could carry out a study to investigate the effectiveness of a marketing campaign. When customers entered a travel agent asking about a holiday, some customers would be randomly selected and offered free insurance for their holiday. The independent variable is whether the customer was offered free insurance, and the dependent variable is whether the customer bought the holiday or not.

We can represent the results of the study in a *contingency table*, as shown in Table 8.4. Of 100 people who were offered free insurance, 65 bought a holiday. Of 100 people who were not offered free insurance, 52 bought a holiday. We are interested in testing the null hypothesis that offering free insurance makes no difference to the probability that someone would buy a holiday.

		Bought a holiday		
		Yes	No	Total
Offered free insurance?	Yes	65	35	100
	No	52	48	100
	Total	117	83	200

Table 8.4: Contingency table.

> **Crucial concept** A χ^2 *(chi-squared) test* is used to compare two or more groups when the dependent variable is nominal.

To test this hypothesis, we carry out a chi-squared test. When you report a χ^2 test, you should report the value for χ^2, the *df* and the associated *p* value. In the case of the data presented in Table 8.4, we find that $\chi^2 = 3.48$, $df = 1$ and $p = 0.062$. So, because the value for *p* is greater than 0.05, we cannot reject the null hypothesis that offering a free holiday does not have any effect on people's purchasing.

The χ^2 test makes the following assumptions of your data:

- *Count each person once only.* Every person must only make one contribution to the contingency table. If they make more than one contribution, the χ^2 is invalid. For example, if our dependent variable was whether the person ate chips or salad, and we counted someone separately under both chips and salad (thus counting that person twice), we could not analyse the data using χ^2.

- *Expected values less than 5.* If you calculate χ^2 by hand, you will calculate expected values. Alternatively, if you use a computer, the expected values should be reported by the computer. For the test to be valid, at least 80% of the expected values in a contingency table must exceed 5. If they do not exceed 5, you can use Fisher's exact test, and if you are suffering from this problem, you need to use a larger sample.

Three or more levels of independent variable

The χ^2 test for a contingency table generalises to a table which has more than two levels of the independent variable and more than two possible outcomes for the dependent variable. We could carry out an experiment further examining people's behaviour in the travel agents. As well as offering them free insurance, we could offer free children's places on the holiday. In addition to just looking at whether they bought a holiday, we could see if they took brochures away or not. Our contingency table for this study would have three rows (offered nothing, free insurance or free child places) and three columns (bought nothing, took brochure away, bought holiday), as in Table 8.5.

		Action			
		Bought nothing	**Took away brochures**	**Bought holiday**	**Total**
	Nothing	105	120	75	300
Offered	Free insurance	85	140	75	300
	Free child places	75	100	125	300
	Total	265	360	275	900

Table 8.5: Contingency table.

The χ^2 value is now equal to 30.1, with 4 df, $p < 0.0001$, and because the p value is less than 0.05, we can reject the null hypothesis that there is no difference between the three conditions of the independent variable.

If you analyse a contingency table which is larger than 2×2 using a χ^2 test, you must still make the assumption that 80% of the expected values are greater than 5. Unfortunately if your table is not a 2×2 table, you cannot carry out a Fisher's exact test. Some computer programs will allow you to do something called an 'exact test', but these are rather complex – the better option is to collect data from a larger sample.

We saw that when we had an interval dependent variable, it was possible to further explore the data using *post hoc* tests. It is possible to further explore the data from a contingency table using *post hoc* tests, but it is difficult and very rarely done – the procedure is described in Everitt (1992).

Within-participants design

TWO LEVELS OF INDEPENDENT VARIABLE

Crucial concept *McNemar's test* and *the sign test* are used in a within-participants experiment which has one independent variable which has two levels and a dependent variable which can take on one of two values.

If you are designing a repeated measures study that has a nominal dependent variable, you are limited in the choices that you can make. The dependent variable must be dichotomous – that is it must only be able to take on two values. If you do not stick to this restriction, you will find it very difficult to analyse your data. There are two similar tests that can be used, the sign test and McNemar's test.

The sign test gives a value of either S or Z (if you calculate it by hand, you will probably use S but most computer programs give Z). It is reported as $Z = 2.69$, $p = 0.007$.

McNemar's test gives a χ^2, and is reported as $\chi^2 = 7.2$, $N = 262$, $p = 0.007$.

THREE OR MORE LEVELS OF INDEPENDENT VARIABLE

If you have a repeated measures design in which there are three levels of the independent variable, you must ensure that the dependent variable is dichotomous – that is, it can only take on one of two values. If the dependent variable is not dichotomous, you can carry out a Cochran's Q test. When you carry out this test you should report Q, the *df* and the p value.

More than one independent variable

Experiments which have a nominal dependent variable and more than one independent variable are very difficult to analyse and it is unlikely that you will cover the appropriate analyses for this in your degree studies.

If you have an independent groups design and more than one independent variable, you need to use loglinear analysis or hierarchical loglinear analysis.

There are no simple techniques to analyse experimental data with a nominal dependent variable when a repeated measures design has been used with more than one independent variable.

Section summary

In this section, we have examined techniques for the analysis of experiments with nominal data. We considered the χ^2 test, McNemar's test, the sign test and Cochran's Q test.

Section 5 Continuous variables – correlation

What are you studying?

In this section we look at the analysis of correlational studies, where we are interested in the relationship between two variables. First, we review scatterplots as a way of examining relationships, then we look at the correlation statistic (*r*). We consider the dual role of a correlation, as both an inferential and a descriptive statistic.

Introduction

> Crucial concept A *correlation* is a measure of the linear relationship (agreement) between two variables.

So far in this chapter we have been looking how data from experiments are analysed. We saw in Chapter 3 that experimental studies are not always appropriate – we might be interested in the relationship between two variables. We can search for natural variation in two or more variables and look for a relationship between them. On some occasions we might consider one of these variables to be the independent variable and one the dependent variable – if we were interested in looking at the relationship between age and beliefs about pre-marital sex, we would consider age to be the independent variable. On other occasions, we do not think of the relationship between two variables as being one of an independent variable and a dependent variable – there is no implication that there is any sort of a causal relationship between our variables, we are just interested in the relationship. Or we might be interested in the relationship between two different measures of intelligence to see if they were measuring the same, or a similar, thing, for example.

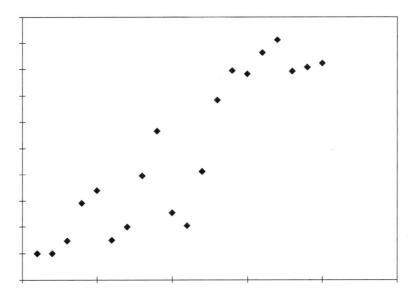

Figure 8.9: A scatterplot showing the relationship between two variables.

If we want to visually examine the relationship between two variables, we can do this on a scatterplot. Figure 8.9 is a scatterplot showing how the relationship between two variables can be plotted, with one point representing one individual being measured.

A correlation tells us two things: it tells us about the *degree* of the relationship between two variables and the *direction* of the relationship between two variables.

Degree of the relationship

A correlation is represented by the correlation coefficient statistic r, which can vary from +1.00 to −1.00. A correlation coefficient of +1.00 or −1.00 indicates a perfect linear relationship. A coefficient near to +1.00 indicates that if A, the first variable goes up, so does B, the second variable.

Figure 8.10 shows a scatterplot that represents a perfect linear relationship between the variables. The correlation in this case is $r = 1.00$, and all of the points lie in a perfectly straight line from the bottom left-hand corner to the top right-hand corner.

Figure 8.11 shows a relationship where the points are further scattered from the perfect relationship but still definitely have a strong relationship. In this case the relationship is $r = 0.9$. Figure 8.12 shows a scatterplot where the points are very scattered, but there is still some trend for them to go from the bottom left to the top right. In this case the correlation is equal to 0.4.

Finally, Figure 8.13 shows a correlation of 0.00. In this case there is no pattern at all, the points are scattered randomly.

Direction of the relationship

The direction of a correlation can be either positive or negative.

- *Positive correlation* occurs when an increase in one variable is accompanied by an increase in the other.

- *Negative correlation* occurs when an increase in one variable is accompanied by a decrease in the other.

A + (positive) or − (negative) sign is used to indicate the direction of the relationship.

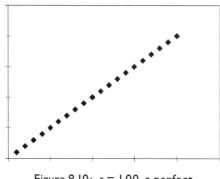

Figure 8.10: $r = 1.00$, a perfect, positive linear relationship.

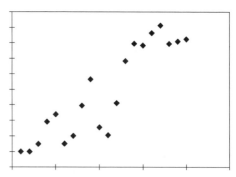

Figure 8.11: $r = 0.90$, a strong, positive relationship. The points all lie close to the diagonal line of a perfect relationship.

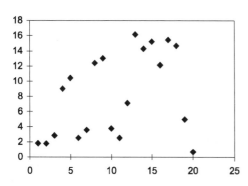

Figure 8.12: $r = 0.40$, a moderate relationship. The points lie near the diagonal but are spread out.

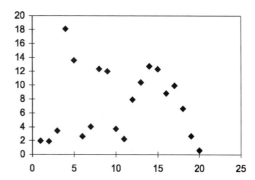

Figure 8.13: $r = 0.00$, no linear relationship. The points are scattered randomly.

Measures of correlation

We will look at the two most common calculations used for correlations: Pearson's product moment correlation and Spearman's rho, which are often shortened to Spearman and Pearson correlations.

PEARSON'S CORRELATION

> Crucial concept A Pearson product moment correlation (usually shortened to *Pearson correlation*) is a parametric measure of agreement between two continuous measures.

The Pearson correlation is the most common form of correlation. This is a parametric test and so makes the standard parametric assumptions:

- normal distribution;
- interval data.

When you report a Pearson correlation you should report the value of r, either df or N, and the probability value.

Crucial concept A Spearman's rho correlation (usually shortened to *Spearman correlation*) is a non-parametric measure of agreement between two ordinal measures.

This is a non-parametric equivalent to the Pearson correlation and is suitable for use with ordinal data or data which are not normally distributed. When reporting a Spearman correlation, you should report the value of r, the N and the associated probability value.

Description and correlations

A correlation is a little curious because it functions in two different ways. It is both a *descriptive* statistic and an *inferential* statistic. It is a descriptive statistic because it tells us something about the relationship between two variables – it is a way of summarising a scatterplot. It is an inferential statistic because you can test the significance of a particular value – that is, you can see if a correlation of that magnitude were likely to occur in your sample, if the null hypothesis – that there is no correlation in the population – were true.

Cohen (1988) defined the standard for assessing the size of correlations. He talked about the size of the effect of one variable on another variable, calling this *effect size*. He said that a correlation of 0.5 was a large effect size, 0.3 is a medium effect size and 0.1 is a small effect size.

Section summary

In this section, we have considered the correlation. A correlation is a way of expressing the linear relationship between two variables. We considered the (parametric) Pearson's correlation, and the (non-parametric) Spearman's correlation.

Further reading

What you should read to learn more depends upon whether the approach taken in your university is to do statistical analysis 'by hand' or whether you use a computer package.

If the approach is to carry out statistics 'by hand' a good book to start off with is *Learning to Use Statistical Tests in Psychology* by Greene and D'Oliveira (Open University Press). A more advanced text, which you should consider looking at whether you use a computer or not, is *Statistical Methods for Psychology* by Howell (published by Wadsworth).

If you are using a computer package to carry out your statistical analysis, you need to consult a book that covers the package that you use. The most common program used by universities is SPSS and so I will mention books that use this – apologies if you are using a different program. Two books which focus mainly on the program and less on the statistics are *SPSS for Psychologists* by Brace, Kemp and Snelgar (published by Sage) and *SPSS for Windows/Macintosh Made Simple* by Kinnear and Gray (published by Erlbaum). If you want a book that focuses more on statistics, and less on the program, then see *Discovering Statistics Using SPSS for Windows* by Field (published by Sage) or *Biostatistics: The Bare Essentials* by Norman and Streiner (published by Decker). Both of these books take a lighthearted approach to statistical analysis.

FURTHER
READING

In this section are listed some books that you might want to look at to further your studies of research methods and statistics in psychology. If there is a book that you think should be here but isn't, please feel free to e-mail me and let me know (details in the preface). A longer, and updated version of this list appears at: http://www.jeremymiles.co.uk/crucial.

Breakwell, G., Hammond, S. and Fife-Schaw, C. (eds) (2000) *Research Methods in Psychology,* 2nd edn. London: Sage. A more advanced text with a focus on a very wide range of research methods, including both quantitative and qualitative approaches.

Coolican, H. (1999) *Research Methods and Statistics in Psychology*, 3rd edn. London: Hodder & Stoughton. A good book to introduce a range of methods – one of the best if you are going to be calculating statistical tests 'by hand'.

Everitt, B. S. and Wykes, T. (1999) *A Dictionary of Statistics for Psychologists*. London: Arnold. This book is exactly what it says on the cover: an accessible dictionary of statistics aimed at psychologists.

Norman, G. R. and Streiner, D. L. (2000) *Biostatistics: The Bare Essentials*. Ontario: Decker. An excellent book for statistics if you are analysing your data using a computer packages. Includes CRAP detectors (i.e. Convoluted Reasoning or Anti-intellectual Pomposity detectors). A rare example of a textbook that manages to be humorous without being irritating.

Pedhazur, E. J. and Schmelkin, L. P. (1991) *Measurement, Design and Analysis: An Integrated Approach*. Hillsdale, NJ: Erlbaum. One of my favourite books – this covers everything, from the beginnings to advanced techniques. Not to everyone's taste though – the authors do not pull any punches when it comes to practices of which they disapprove.

The Sage 'Little Green Books' (Quantitative Applications in the Social Sciences). If you are interested in a specific technique, the publisher Sage produces a series of small books each focusing on a specific technique. At the time of writing there are 135 books in the series.

Smithson, M. (2000) *Statistics with Confidence*. London: Sage. A nice second-level statistics text book – go for this if you are looking for a bit more detail, but not too much more.

Tabachnick, B. and Fidell, L. (2000) *Using Multivariate Statistics*, 4th edn. New York: Allyn & Bacon. This is a book to go for if you are looking for a text that covers the more advanced, multivariate statistics. Not for beginners though.

REFERENCES

Abelson, R. P. (1995) *Statistics as Principled Argument*. Hillsdale, NJ: Erlbaum.

American Psychological Association (1994) *Publication Manual of the American Psychological Association*, 4th edn. Washington, DC: APA.

Anastasi, A. and Urbina, S. (1997) *Psychological testing*, 7th edn. New York: Prentice Hall.

APA (2001) *Publication manual of the American Psychological Association*, 5th edn. Washington: American Psychological Association.

Aronson, E., Ellsworth, P. C., Carlsmith, J. M. and Gonzales, M. H. (1989) *Methods of research in social psychology*, 2nd edn.. New York: McGraw Hill.

Barlow, J. and Harrison, K. (1996) Focusing on empowerment: facilitating self-help in young people with arthritis through a disability organization. *Disability and Society, 11*, 539-551.

Bell, P., Staines, P., and Mitchell, J. (2001) *Evaluating, Doing and Writing Research*. Thousand Oaks, CA: Sage.

Bond, R. and Smith, P. B. (1996) 'Culture and conformity: a meta-analysis of studies using Asch's […] line judgment task', *Psychological Bulletin*, 119, 111–37.

Brace, N., Kemp, R. and Snelgar, R. (2000) *SPSS for Psychologists*. Basingstoke: Palgrave.

British Psychological Society (2000) *Code of Conduct, Ethical Principles and Guidelines*. Leicester: British Psychological Society.

Cardwell, M. (1999) *Ethical Issues in Psychology*. London: Routledge.

Chow, S. L. (1996) *Statistical Significance*. Thousand Oaks, CA: Sage.

Cohen, J. (1988) *Statistical Power Analysis for the Behavioral Sciences*. Hillsdale, NJ: Erlbaum.

Cook, T. D. and Campbell, D. T. (1979) *Quasi-experimentation: Design and Analysis Issues for Field Settings*. Boston: Houghton-Mifflin.

Cronbach, L. J. (1951) 'Coefficient alpha and the internal structure of tests', *Psychometrika*, 16, 297–334.

Cronbach, L. J. and Meehl, P. E. (1955) 'Construct validity in psychological tests', *Psychological Bulletin*, 52, 281–302.

Cusick, L. (1998) 'Female prostitution in Glasgow: drug use and occupational sector', *Addiction Research*, 6, 115–30.

DeCarlo, L. T. (1997) 'On the meaning and use of kurtosis', *Psychological Methods*, 2, 292–307.

Everitt, B. S. (1992) *The Analysis of Contingency Tables*. London: Chapman & Hall.

Eysenck, H. J. (1967) *The Biological Basis of Personality*. Springfield, IL: Charles C. Thomas.

Eysenck, H. J. (1985) *Decline and Fall of the Freudian Empire*. London: Penguin.

Festinger, L. , Riecken, H. W. and Schachter, S. (1956) *When Prophecy Fails*. New York: Harper & Row.

Field, A. (2000) *Discovering Statistics Using SPSS*. London: Sage.

Fink, A. (ed.) (1995) *The Survey Kit*. Thousand Oaks, CA: Sage

Fink, A. (1995) *How to Ask Survey Questions*. London: Sage.

Fisher, S. (1999) 'A prevalence study of gambling and problem gambling in British adolescents', *Addiction Research*, 7, 509–38.

Gale, A. (1973) 'The psychophysiology of individual differences: studies of extraversion and the EEG', in P. Kline (ed.), *New Approaches in Psychological Measurement*. London: John Wiley & Sons.

Gerrards-Hesse, A. , Spies, K. and Hesse, W. (1994) 'Experimental inductions of emotional states and their effectiveness: an overview', *British Journal of Psychology*, 85, 55–78.

Goldstein, H., Rasbash, J., Yang, M., Woodhouse, G., Pan, H., Nuttall, D. and Thomas, S. (1993) 'A multilevel analysis of school examination results', *Oxford Review of Education*, 19, 425–33.

Greene and D'Oliveira (2000) *Learning to Use Statistical Tests in Psychology*, 2nd edn. Milton Keynes: Open University Press.

Griffiths, M. (1997) 'Exercise addiction: a case study', *Addiction Research*, 5, 161–8.

Harlow, L., Mulaik, S. A. and Steiger, J. (1997) *What If There Were No Significance Tests*. Hillsdale, NJ: Erlbaum

Heiman, G. (1998) *Research Methods in Psychology*. Boston, MA: Houghton Mifflin.

Herrnstein, R. J. and Murray, C. (1994) *The Bell Curve: Intelligence and Class Structure in American Life*. New York: Free Press.

Howell, D.C. (1997) *Statistical Methods for Psychology*, 4th edn. Belmont, CA: Duxbury.

Huff, D. (1954/1999) *How To Lie With Statistics*. London: Penguin.

Jones, J. L. (1995) *Understanding Psychological Science*. New Jersey: Prentice Hall.

Kendall, P. C. and Flannery-Schroeder, E. C. (1995) 'Rigor, but not rigor mortis in depression research', *Journal of Personality and Social Psychology*, 68, 892–4.

Keren, G. (1993) 'Between or within subjects design: a methodological dilemma', in G. Keren and C. Lewis (eds), *A Handbook for Data Analysis in the Behavioral Sciences: Methodological Issues*. Hillsdale, NJ: Erlbaum.

Keren, G. and Lewis, C. (1993) *Handbook for Data Analysis in the Behavioural Sciences: Methodological Issues*. Hillsdale, NJ: Erlbaum.

Kimmel, A. J. (1996) *Ethical Issues in Behavioural Research*. Oxford: Blackwell.

Kinnear, P. R. and Gray, C. D. (2000) *SPSS for Windows Made Simple*, 3rd edn. Hove: Psychology Press.

Kline, P. (1981) *Fact and Fantasy in Freudian Theory*. London: Routledge.

Kosslyn, S. (1993) *Elements of Graph Design*. New York: WH Freeman.

Kraemer, H. C. and Theimann, S. (1987) *How Many Subjects: Statistical Power and Analysis in Research*. London: Sage.

Levin, I. P. (1999) *Relating Statistics and Experimental Design*. Thousand Oaks, CA: Sage.

Loehlin, J. C. (1992) *Genes and Environment in Personality Development*. London: Sage.

Mcghee, P. (2001) *Thinking Psychologically*. Basingstoke: Palgrave.

Miles, J. N. V. and Shevlin, M. (2001) *Applying Regression and Correlation: A Guide for Students and Researchers*. London: Sage.

Milgram, S. (1974/1997) *Obedience to Authority*. London: Pinter and Martin.

Mohr, L. B. (1990) *Understanding Significance Testing*. Thousand Oaks, CA: Sage.

Norman, G.R. and Streiner, D.L. (2000) *Biostatistics: the Bare Essentials*. Ontario, Canada: Decker.

Nunnally, J. C. and Bernstein, I. H. (1994) *Psychometric Theory*, 3rd edn. New York: McGraw-Hill.

Oppenheim, A. N. (2000) *Questionnaire Design and Attitude Measurement.* London: Continuum.

Orne, M. T. (1962) 'On the social psychology of the psychological experiment: with particular reference to demand characteristics and their implications', *American Psychologist*, 17, 776–83.

Pearl, J. (2000) *Causality: Models, Reasoning and Inference.* Cambridge: Cambridge University Press.

Polledri, P. (1997) 'Forensic psychotherapy with a potential serial killer', *British Journal of Psychotherapy*, 13, 473–88.

Riemann, R., Grubich, C., Hempel, S., Mergl, S. and Richter, M. (1993) 'Personality and attitudes towards current political topics', *Personality and Individual Differences*, 15, 313–21.

Rind, B. (1996) 'Effect of beliefs about weather conditions on tipping', *Journal of Applied Social Psychology*, 26, 137–47.

Robson, C. (1993) *Real World Research.* Oxford: Blackwell.

Rosnow, R. L. and Rosenthal, R. (1997) *People Studying People: Artifacts and Ethics in Behavioral Research.* New York: WH Freeman.

Simpson, E. H. (1951) 'The interpretation of interaction in contingency tables', *Journal of the Royal Statistical Society, Series B*, 13, 238–41.

Stevens, S. S. (1946) 'On the theory of scales of measurement', *Science*, 103, 677–80.

Stevens, S. S. (1951) 'Mathematics, measurement, and psychophysics', in S. S. Stevens (ed.), *Handbook of Experimental Psychology*. New York: John Wiley & Sons.

Strunk, W. and White, S. (2000) *The Elements of Style*, 3rd edn. New York: Allyn and Bacon.

Taylor, C. R. and Stern, B. B. (1997) 'Asian-Americans: television advertising and the "model minority" stereotype', *Journal of Advertising*, 26, 47–61.

Tennen, H., Hall, J. A. and Affleck, G. (1995) 'Depression research methodologies in the JPSP: a review and critique', *Journal of Personality and Social Psychology*, 68, 870–84.

Townsend, S. (1984) *The Growing Pains of Adrian Mole*. London: Mandarin.

Wareing, M., Fisk, J. E. and Murphy, P. N. (2000) 'Working memory deficits in current and previous users of MDMA ("ecstasy")', *British Journal of Psychology*, 91, 181–8.

Weary, G., Edwards, J. and Jacobson, J. A. (1995) 'Depression research methodologies in the JPSP: a reply', *Journal of Personality and Social Psychology*, 68, 885–91.

Wulfert, E., Safren, S. A., Brown, I. and Wan, C. K. (1999) 'Cognitive, behavioral, and personality correlates of HIV-positive persons' unsafe sexual behavior', *Journal of Applied Social Psychology*, 29, 223–44.

INDEX

Crucial Study Guides for Psychology Degree Courses

Titles in the series

Biopsychology	ISBN 1 903337 12 7	Price £9.99
Cognitive Psychology	ISBN 1 903337 13 5	Price £9.99
Developmental Psychology	ISBN 1 903337 14 3	Price £9.99
History and Philosophy of Psychology	ISBN 1 903337 17 8	Price £9.99
Research Methods and Statistics	ISBN 1 903337 15 1	Price £9.99
Social Psychology	ISBN 1 903337 16 X	Price £9.99

To order, please contact our distributors:

Plymbridge Distributors, Estover Road, Plymouth, PL6 7PY
Tel: 01752 202301. Fax: 01752 202333. Email: orders@plymbridge.com
www.plymbridge.com